fashionable clothing
from the sears catalogs

MID
1930s

Tammy Ward

Schiffer Publishing Ltd.

4880 Lower Valley Road Atglen, Pennsylvania 19310

Designed by John P. Cheek
Cover design by Bruce Waters
Type set in Zurich BT

ISBN: 978-0-7643-2734-6
Printed in China

Published by Schiffer Publishing Ltd.
4880 Lower Valley Road
Atglen, PA 19310
Phone: (610) 593-1777; Fax: (610) 593-2002
E-mail: Info@schifferbooks.com

For the largest selection of fine reference books on this and related subjects, please visit our web site at **www.schifferbooks.com**
We are always looking for people to write books on new and related subjects. If you have an idea for a book please contact us at the above address.

This book may be purchased from the publisher.
Include $3.95 for shipping.
Please try your bookstore first.
You may write for a free catalog.

In Europe, Schiffer books are distributed by
Bushwood Books
6 Marksbury Ave.
Kew Gardens
Surrey TW9 4JF England
Phone: 44 (0) 20 8392-8585; Fax: 44 (0) 20 8392-9876
E-mail: info@bushwoodbooks.co.uk
Website: www.bushwoodbooks.co.uk
Free postage in the U.K., Europe; air mail at cost.

Contents

Introduction

As you browse through the pages of this book, you will see many styles that are Autographed Fashions worn in Hollywood by the stars of the mid 1930s. Hollywood had a large impact on the fashions of this era. Many styles were endorsed by movie stars, such as Helen Twelvetrees, Loretta Young, Ginger Rogers, Frances Dee, Fay Wray, Anita Louise, Lilian Boud, Mary Brian, Joan Marsh, Joan Bennett, Adrienne Ames, and Dorothy Wilson, among others. Endorsements from the stars were a common occurrence. Movie stars and people of royalty became adored fashion icons. Women demanded to have the same fashions and products as the stars so that they too could dress in glamorous allure.

Sun bathing became a passion and women showed off their tans with full-length, backless evening dresses cut on the true cross or bias that molded the body. A slim figure was essential for this look too. Women who were educated began using contraception to avoid bearing a child, unless that is what they wanted. They began to have a choice in motherhood. Also essential to the popular slim look was a bra. In 1935 the bust cup sizes A, B, C, and D were introduced by Warners.

During the 1930s, a fashion "must-have" was animal fur. Pelts in high demand at this time were mink, chinchilla, sable, silver fox, and Persian lamb.

In 1935 the DuPont de Nemours Company successfully synthesized nylon threads; therebysee-through nylon stockings also became exciting fashion accessory "must-haves."

Men's fashion styles also followed what actors in Hollywood were wearing. It is said that men began to do away with their undershirts simply because Clark Gable took off his shirt in a movie and showed only his bare chest. The double-breasted suit also became popular. Masculine elegance was found in jackets with long, broad lapels. Trousers were generously cut. Popular colors for suits were midnight or navy blue, charcoal, and gray. Suits were enhanced by herringbone and vertical and diagonal stripes.

Plaids became popular during this time and could be found on fabrics such as tweed, cheviot, and wool. The blazer was the garment of choice for casual wear. It was worn with long slacks or shorts.

Fashions for men, women, and children are shown throughout this book. Take a stroll back in time to an era heavily influenced by Hollywood's movie stars. Historians and designers alike will delight in the fashions of the mid-1930s.

Accessories

Bright scarves will brighten up any outfit. *Spring & Summer 1935*

Matching hat and scarf set will glorify any plain outfit. *Fall & Winter 1934*

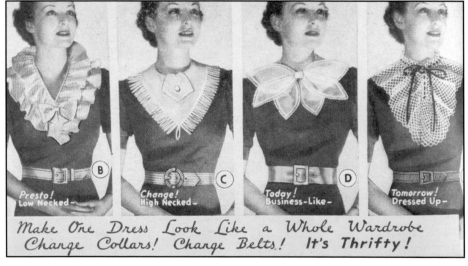

Change collars and belts to enhance and change your wardrobe!
Spring & Summer 1935

A variety of collars that look stunning against dark dresses. *Fall & Winter 1935-1936*

Tailored Flared Tops in Fine Selected Kidskin

$195

A Pair

—Lightweight kidskin
—About 4½-button length slipons —Overseam sewed

Fashion favors this flared cuff style with its light scalloped edge and raised seaming outlined in contrast stitching. Smart! You can see their quality at a glance. Beautifully tailored by one of Europe's leading makers. Quality you can't duplicate under $3.00. Contrasting stitching on backs. Imported from Germany.

33 K 3010—Black **33 K 3011**—Brown
33 K 3012—Navy Blue

Quarter sizes, 6 to 8. State size wanted.
Shipping weight, 4 ounces.

$175
A Pair

Our Finest Capeskin
SHIRRED WRIST STRAP

—Our best imported lightweight capeskin
—About 3¾-button length —Overseam sewed
—Table cut for perfect fit

These strike a new note! Extra fine slip on snugged at the wrist with a narrow leather strap

Kidskin and Capeskin fashionable gloves. *Fall & Winter 1935-1936*

Block knit cotton set has peaked hat and scarf. Pompon tam and turtle-neck bib are rib-knit all wool yarn. Hand draped turban and matching scarf in multi-colored knit cotton. *Fall & Winter 1935-1936*

Autographed by *Adrienne Ames*

Bemberg Ruffsuede

Gloves autographed by Adrienne Ames in Bemberg Ruffsuede. *Fall & Winter 1935-1936*

7

Aprons, Utility, Uniforms

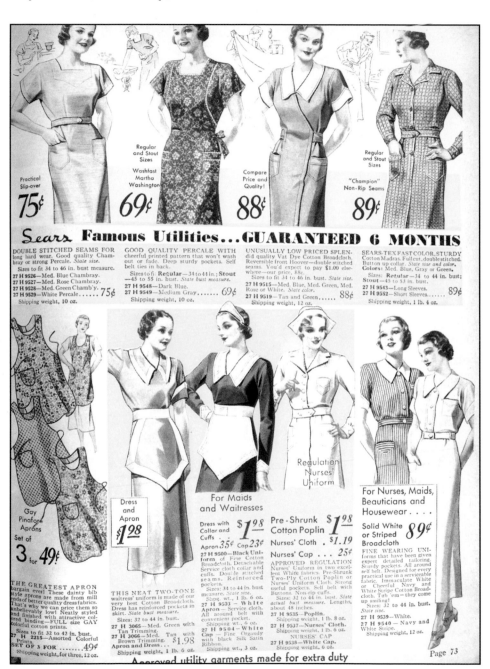

Sears-Tex work dresses stands up under the hardest wear. *Fall & Winter 1935-1936*

A variety of utility wear for women who need to get a job done. *Spring & Summer 1935*

Casual Separates

Pique Surplice Blouse
1.19

Part-Wool Skirt
$1.19

Regular and Stout Sizes

Your Initial! Silk Satin Slip-over
85¢

Sports Skirt
89¢

Gingham Blouse
69¢

Tweed Skirt
$1.15

Navy Slacks
$1.29

Knit Sports Shirt
59¢

White Slacks
95¢

Blouses, skirts, and slacks to mix and match for casual wear. *Spring & Summer 1935*

PJs, Robes and Loungewear

Shop SEARS FIRST FOR BATHROBES AND NEGLIGEES

ALL WOOL FLANNEL
$3.98
E

D
SATIN BROCADE RAYON TWILL
$2.98

D Luxuriously lovely and priced so low. Glowing, lustrous Satin Brocade All Rayon Twill in exquisite flower shades, fashioned this beauty. Trimmed with self color all rayon twill Satin.

Sizes: Small (34-36); Medium (38-40); Large (42-44) in. bust measure. State size and color.
31 F 4909—Orchid, Medium Blue or Rose. Each........ $2.98

Sent direct from New York to you... but you pay the postage only from our nearest Mail Order Store.
Shpg. Wt., 1 lb. 4 oz.

F
For the Beach or Lazy days around the house
$1.79

F Just the robe for summer wear, for it is made of superior quality Fruit-of-the-Loom Checked Cotton that washes beautifully. Heavy enough to tailor perfectly in full, swagger lines, with generous over lap. Looks

Robes in satin brocade rayon twill, all wool flannel, and Fruit-of-the-Loom checked cotton. *Spring & Summer 1934*

Ideal Gifts

F
Special! all wool flannel
$2.98
ALSO IN part wool flannel
$2.29

G
Warm, Comfy double-ombre Genuine BEACON Blanket Robe
$3.39

H
Popular double breasted model in fine all wool flannel
$4.39

Sears Robes are full long lengths with generous overlaps.

J
The Perfect Gift
lovely all rayon twill
$2.77

we all need a mid-weight *Washable* robe like this
$1.98

K

L
Your Choice solid color or patterned blanket cloth
Our Bargain Value! $1.79 EACH

L Good quality, medium weight Cotton Blanket Cloth robes. Soft, warm and sturdy. Full sizes. Rayon cord edging and girdle. State actual size. Sizes to fit 34 to 44 inches bust measure.
PATTERN BLANKET ROBE
27 F 3260—Medium Rose.
27 F 3261—Lavender.
27 F 3262—Medium Blue...............$1.79
SOLID COLORS
27 F 3265—Medium Rose.
27 F 3266—Medium Green.
27 F 3267—Medium Blue...............$1.79
weight, each, 2 lbs., 4 oz.

A selection of lovely long robes with generous overlaps. *Fall & Winter 1934*

Balbriggans knit pajamas are the newest in warm healthful fashions. *Fall & Winter 1934*

Cotton crinkle crepe and cotton flannel pajamas for cold winter nights. *Fall & Winter 1934*

Women's robes, hostess frock, and Japanese lounging robe. *Spring & Summer 1935*

Rayon pajamas and gowns. *Spring & Summer 1935*

Amoskeag cotton flannel tuck-in pajamas. *Fall & Winter 1935-1936*

All wool flannel robes for big and little girls. *Fall & Winter 1935-1936*

Coats

Harris-type tweed coat in wool, rayon, and cotton. Hairy surfaced Harris-type tweed coat with a collar that can be worn closed. Homespun weave tweed coat has the newest sleeves and collar for 1934! *Spring & Summer 1934*

For the junior miss, "Movie Star", "Knockabout", "Sportster", and "Sunday Best" are all the newest style in this season's coats. *Spring & Summer 1934*

Botany woolen coats in long slim lines are silk lined and have the newest style collars. *Spring & Summer 1936*

Fishtail swagger coat is one of New York's newest fashions in smart looking plaid. Very swank! *Spring & Summer 1936*

White coats in the latest styles include a polo, Angora Rabbit hair, Stroller, and a swagger made of cotton cord lace. *Spring & Summer 1936*

White swagger coat with big patch pockets and raglan sleeves. White novelty weave coat has the new high neckline, and big buttons. White coat with frog fastening that looks just like expensive flannel. *Spring & Summer 1936*

Genuine mink-dyed marmot fur coat with wool Crepolaine, Lapin Coney fir with all wool broadcloth, and gorgeous Astrakhan fur fabric with genuine silver-pointed wolf-dyed Manchurian dog fur. *Fall & Winter 1934*

Genuine wolf-dyed Manchurian dog fur on all wool crepe coating is splendidly tailored. *Fall & Winter 1934*

Imagine!

GENUINE WOLF-DYED MANCHURIAN DOG FUR

ALL WOOL CREPE COATING

$9⁷⁵

Splendidly Big collar o churian' Do Lined with about 48¼
Misses' Si Women's bust measur
17 F 5070—
17 F 5071—
Shipping w

MUFF of W
17 F 5797—
Shipping w

Genuine Furs Fine Fabrics

IN THESE SEARS NEW YORK-STYLED COAT FASHIONS

Every one a Marvelous Value!

Fine
ALL WOOL CREPE COATING
SILK LINED

ALSO IN SPECIAL SIZES for the Short Woman

SILVER POINTED WOLF-DYED MANCHURIAN DOG FUR

$13⁹⁵

WITH BLACK WOLF-DYED MANCHURIAN DOG FUR

$12⁹⁵

Here's style, quality, value! One of our special leaders in a better coat. Fine quality All Wool Crepe coating, tailored in slim, flattering figure lines. Smart tie-belt. Good quality Silk Crepe (weighted) lining. Warm interlining. Luxurious big, full collar of gleaming genuine Wolf-dyed Manchurian Dog Fur. State actual bust measure—make no allowance.
Misses' Sizes: 14-16-18-20 years.
Women's Sizes: 32-34-36-38-40-42 and 44 inches bust measure. Lengths, about 48½ inches.
17 F 5145—Black with Silver Pointed Fur........ $13.95
17 F 5148—Black with Black Fur................. $12.95
Short Women's Sizes: 34-36-38-40 and 42 inches bust measure. Lengths, about 46 inches. State actual bust measure.
17 F 5440—Black with Silver Pointed Fur........ $13.95
17 F 5443—Black with Black Fur................. $12.95
Send your order direct to New York. See Page 4.
Shipping weight, each 4 lbs. 14 oz.

Flattering—
NEW COLLAR OF FLUFFY TUSCANY MANDEL FUR

ALL WOOL CREPE COATING

$12⁹⁸

Fur—soft, long haired, densely thick genuine Tuscany Mandel in richly dyed coloring. Raccoon Shade on Brown and Badger dye on Black, fashions this handsome collar with its smart, ripple revers. Superior quality All Wool Crepe Coating lends itself gracefully to the tailored panel seamings that give that gorgeous slim silhouette. Sleeves attractively tucked. A belt is sent with the coat—wear it with or without to suit your figure. Rayon and Cotton lining over warm interlining. A great value coat, a stunning style! State actual bust measure—make no allowance.
Misses' Sizes: 16-18-20 years.
Women's Sizes: 34-36-38-40-42-44-46 in. bust measure. Lengths, about 48½ inches.
17 F 5150—Medium Dark Brown.
17 F 5151—Black........................... $12.98
Send your order direct to New York. See Page 4.
Shipping weight, 5 lbs.

SILKY RICH BEAVER-DYED FRENCH CONEY FUR

$16⁹⁵

Excellent Quality TREE BARK COATING
SILK LINED

Fashion's newest fabric and it's sturdy, warm, All Wool. Soft, lustrous, Beaver-Dyed genuine French Coney Fur on Brown and Green, Black Seal dye on Black, fashions the gorgeous big collar. Flower included. Silk Crepe (weighted) lining with good warm interlining. State actual bust measure—make no allowance.
Misses' Sizes: 16-18-20 years.
Women's Sizes: 34-36-38-40-42-44 in. bust measure. Lengths, about 48½ inches.
17 F 5140—Medium Dark Brown.
17 F 5141—Black.
17 F 5142—Medium Dark Green........ $16.95
Send your order direct to New York. See Page 4.
Shipping weight, 4 lbs. 12 oz.

All wool Crepe coat with silver-pointed wolf-dyed Manchurian dog fur, Silky rich beaver-dyed French Coney fur coat, and flattering new collar of fluffy Tuscany Mandel fur on all wool crepe. *Fall & Winter 1934*

Belgian lynx-dyed Coney fur on wool crepe coat, blue fox-dyed Vicuna fur on fine wool, and all wool broadcloth with genuine Caracul fur come direct to you from New York. *Fall & Winter 1934*

Autographed fashion sports coat worn in Hollywood by Ginger Rogers is the raciest, sassiest coat in Hollywood this year. *Spring & Summer 1935*

Autographed fashion worn in Hollywood by Lilian Boud and thousands of other modern young women! *Spring & Summer 1935*

$12 \underline{75}$

FOR BEAUTY-
FUR EDGE

Real Fur!
All Wool!
Silk Lined!

Genuine Vicuna fur dyed blue fox collar on all wool worsted Crepe is an auto-graphed fashion worn in Hollywood by Loretta Young. *Spring & Summer 1935*

An
Outstanding
Value!

Fine
Crepolaine
with
Real Fur

$9 \underline{95}$

Plaid
With New
Wide Belt

$7 \underline{98}$
All
Wool

"Fawnlam" fur fabric jacket is light and smart, just the thing for spring wear. *Spring & Summer 1935*

Genuine Vicuna fur cuffs adorn this fine Crepolaine coat with fancy collar buttons. Scottish plaid coat is all wool with a wide youthful belt. *Spring & Summer 1935*

17

Adorable "Bunny" jacket.
Spring & Summer 1935

Both Styles also in Special Sizes for **SHORT WOMEN**

All Wool Homespun
$8⁷⁵

Fine Crepe Coating
$7⁹⁵

Coats in all wool or glorious Crepe. *Spring & Summer 1935*

F Swagger Length   All White or Checked **G**

White coats in Honeycomb Weave is a summer necessity.
Spring & Summer 1935

Trimmed with
Stitched Taffeta

Ⓐ

Fine
Crepolaine
$8⁹⁸

Ⓑ
All
Wool
Bark-
Weave
Worsted
$10⁹⁸

Tucked
Revers
are
Smart

Ⓒ
CRE
RIT
$8

With
Flatter
Ripp
Coll

Trimline slimming coats for larger women in fine Crepolaine, all wool bark weave worsted, and Crepe Ritz fabrics. *Spring & Summer 1935*

Trimline coat in all wool tree bark with genuine kidskin fur. 2-piece suit has long coat and skirt with kick pleats. *Spring & Summer 1935*

All Wool
Tree
Bark
with
Genuine
Kidskin
Fur

Our Best Coat
$13⁹⁸

$8⁹⁵

A SUIT
That
Slenderizes

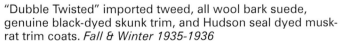

Chevron tweed fabric suit has a matching coat topped with genuine gray wolf fur. An autographed fashion worn in Hollywood by Helen Twelvetrees, this all wool bark weave crepe coat has a button up vestee and the collar hs genuine Dymka fox dyed "wildcat" fur. *Fall & Winter 1935-1936*

"Dubble Twisted" imported tweed, all wool bark suede, genuine black-dyed skunk trim, and Hudson seal dyed musk-rat trim coats. *Fall & Winter 1935-1936*

Deep rayon and cotton pile fabric reproduces genuine Broadtail fur in this jacket. Heavyweight cotton pile fabric jacket that everyone will think is Lapin fur. *Fall & Winter 1935-1936*

FASHION ACES

with Fine New Fabrics, Genuine Furs, and Silk Linings, that put them in the Luxury Class!

Choice $14.95 **Each**

Descriptions on Opposite Page

Ⓒ Smart Ripple Collars

Ⓓ MUFF 3⁹⁸

Ⓐ Genuine Wolf-Dyed Jackal Fur

MUFF 3⁹⁸

Ⓑ Our Best Wolf Dyed Manchurian Dog Fur

Both also in Sizes For Short Women

Ⓔ Genuine Mink-Dyed Marmot Fur

Ⓕ Fine Calf Swagger Bags "Zip" Fitted 1⁹⁴

Ⓖ GAY SCARF 88¢

Sears 41

Fine new fabrics with genuine furs and silk linings. These coats are in a luxury class. *Fall & Winter 1935-1936*

A Joy To Own, Sears **FINEST**
DRESS COATS!

• With Luxurious Furs!
• Lambs' Wool Interlining!
• Smart, New Woolens!
• Silk Crepe Back Satin Linings!

Genuine Fitch Fur

Also comes in sizes for short women

Fine Quality Vicuna Fur

Both in All Wool Bark Suede Fabric

$24.75 $19.98

It's a gorgeous All Wool Bark Suede coating with a lavish collar of genuine Fitch Fur—all selected fine skins with beautiful colorings. We have...

You'd shop Fifth Avenue over and over to find such a stunning coat at this price. It's Fine All Wool Suede coating, (weighted)...

An autographed fashion coat worn in Hollywood by Marian Marsh, in all wool bark suede with genuine wolf fur trim. Two coats in all wool bark suede fabric with genuine Fitch or Vicuna fur collars. *Fall & Winter 1935-1936*

Right:
All wool bark crepe coat is silk lined and has gorgeous blue fox dye on a removable cape. *Fall & Winter 1935-1936*

Far right:
Superb quality fur coats in truly luxurious furs, fabrics, linings, and tailoring. *Fall & Winter 1935-1936*

22

3 AMAZING VALUES! 9^{95} EACH

All in New Bark Weave Fabrics

Rich Fluffy Mandel

Beaver Dyed Coney

Silk Lined

A coat with the air of a much more expensive one. Collar of fluffy rich Mandel Fur, made with the new front fullness and wide revers. The fabric is a new rich Bark Weave C...

Note the smart shaped collar in this lovely coat. It is of fine quality genuine Beaver dyed Coney Fur usually found on higher priced coats. Here again we have tailored this coat with one of the...

Genuine Wolf Dyed Manchurian Dog Fur—Famous for its flattery and long wear.

Genuine Black Caracul—trim youthful loveliness in its...

Bark Weave Crepe coat has rich, fluffy Mandel fur. Bark Weave Crepe coat has beaver dyed Coney. Tree Bark Crepe coat with genuine wolf dyed Manchurian dog fur. *Fall & Winter 1935-1936*

These coats look like the real thing. Cotton fur coat looks like expensive Lapin and has a contrasting pelt. Wool and rayon pile looks like Persian Lamb. Rayon pile looks like Caracul fur with a stand up frill collar. *Fall & Winter 1935-1936*

Ⓐ **Blocked Lapin Fur Fabric** 7^{75}

Astrakhan Fur Fabric $^{\$}9^{75}$

Ⓑ **"Zip" Muff** 1^{19}

Ⓒ **Bloused Back! Caracul Fur Fabric** 9^{95}

You'll Love the Richness Of these Warm FUR-LIKE COATS

Ⓐ A coat that looks like expensive blocked Lapin! Rich and furry! It's *Cozy Pelt*, a thick, deep-piled cotton fur fabric. Luxuriously soft; very durable. Collar of contrast color Cozy Pelt. Warm cotton suede cloth lining.
Misses' Sizes: 14-16-18-20 years.
Women's Sizes: 32-34-36-38-40-42-44 inches bust. Lengths, about 49 inches. *State bust.*
7 K 4142—Beige Tan with Brown. $7.75
7 K 4144—Brown with Beige Tan.
Shipping weight, 5 lbs. 8 oz.

Stylish and Warm Astrakhan Cloth
The tight curly-napped fur fabric that gives the effect of Persian Lamb! In a stunning style! Full jabot shawl collar; novelty sleeves. Wool and Rayon pile with a sturdy cotton back. Lined with Fancy Rayon and cotton. Interlined. *State bust measure.*
Misses' Sizes: 14-16-18-20 years.
Women's Sizes: 32-34-36-38-40-42-44-46 in. bust. Lengths, about 49 inches.
7 K 4145—Black.
7 K 4146—Dark Brown. $9.75
Shipping weight, 6 lbs. 8 oz.

Astrakhan Cloth Muff to Match
Sold separately. Pocketbook type with purse and mirror. Zipper closing. Lined with Rayon and cotton.
7 K 4791—Black. $1.19
7 K 4792—Dark Brown.
Shipping weight, 1 lb. 4 oz.

Ⓒ Brand new! A stand-up collar with a frill! The low armhole! The blouse back! Caracul Fur Fabric! Gleaming Rayon pile with a sturdy cotton back—very warm! imitation leather belt. Lined with Rayon and cotton. Warmly interlined. *State bust measure.*
Misses' Sizes: 14-16-18-20 years.
Women's Sizes: 32-34-36-38-40-42 in. bust. Lengths, about 49 inches.
7 K 4148—Rich Black. $9.95
Shipping weight, 4 lbs. 8 oz.

...this page are shipped direct from New York to you ...pay postage only from our nearest Mail Order House.

Genuine wolf-dyed Manchurian dog fur on good crepe coating.
Chinchilla coat has a big collar and smart wide revers. *Fall & Winter 1935-1936*

All wool Melton coat with stitched wide lapels and a big collar. Heavy crepe coat with Mandel ripple fur collar. Crepeolaine coat with genuine wold-dyed black Manchurian dog fur collar. Heavy flecked coat with cozy pelt cotton fur collar. *Fall & Winter 1935-1936*

Glorious 3-piece top coat and suit combination has a slit skirt, button up high jacket, and coat is made in a straight line. Fabric is flecked Chevron weave. *Fall & Winter 1935-1936*

Swagger coat in short haired genuine African Kidskin. Blocked style coat in genuine Lapin fur. *Fall & Winter 1935-1936*

A
SWAGGER!
Genuine
African
Kidskin
59.00

B
Blocked
Genuine
Lapin
39.50

The coats on this page are sent direct from New York to you, but you pay postage only from our nearest Mail Order House.

PREMIER Banded
NORTHERN
BEAVER-DYED-CONEY

The Luxury of

Stunning suit has an un-lined swagger coat, and a hemmed skirt with checked pattern in warm tweed. Fur trimmed suit has genuine Mouflon fur on the cuffs and a hemmed skirt in winter weight tweed fabric. *Fall & Winter 1935-1936*

All wool tree bark weave coat with your choice of black seal-dyed or beaver-dyed Coney fur collar. All wool coat with genuine black Caracul fur collar. *Fall & Winter 1935-1936*

Genuine
Caracul
Fur Trim
ALL WOOL
BROADCLOTH
19.75

F
Luxurious
Fur Collar
$16.95

G
All Wool
Crepe
$17.98

Dresses

Career

Our Best Treebark Suiting! Silk Lined! Piqué Vestee!
$10⁹⁸

3-Piece— Cape comes off!
$9²⁵

Novelty Bark Weave

Suits with capes and coats features bark weave, fur, and lots of style. *Spring & Summer 1935*

Nubby Tweed or Mo... S...
$3⁹⁸

Smart Spring Tweed
$6⁹⁸
Ⓒ

Crepolaine with Pique'Vest
$7²⁵
Ⓓ

Ⓔ

Suits—Tailored to a "T"— at *Sears* exciting, low prices!

Short coat tailored suits in smart spring tweed, crepolaine, and nubby tweed. Long coat suit in diagonal weave. *Spring & Summer 1935*

Casual

These lovely dresses are an autographed fashion worn in Hollywood by Helen Twelvetrees. *Spring & Summer 1936*

"Searspride" frocks in gingham patterns. *Spring & Summer 1936*

Cotton dresses in plaids, stripes, or prints with plain styles. *Spring & Summer 1935*

Sheer dotted cotton Batiste with pleated white organdy trim with grosgrain ribbon bow and belt. Fashion-right stripe cotton pique dress with white cotton pique jacket. *Spring & Summer 1935*

Cotton and percale printed dress. *Spring & Summer 1935*

Full length, full cut daytime frocks in fine cotton prints. *Spring & Summer 1935*

Rayon ruff crepe tunic blouse and pleated skirt. Cotton knit blouse and skirt. Snowfleck cotton suit with silk pongee blouse. *Fall & Winter 1935-1936*

Dressy

4^{98}

Pebble crepe jacket dress with polka dotted scarf and belt is beautifully tailored to accent a slim waistline. *Spring & Summer 1936*

Pure dye all rayon Canton Crepe dress in plain and print combination. *Spring & Summer 1934*

Smart Moderns

Prefer Dresses in Pebble Crepe
Woven of Rich Celanese Yarns

★

There's a Real Sample on Page 304
Feel its Texture . . . See its Beauty!

SIZE AND LENGTH SCALE

Misses' Sizes: 14-16-18-20
To fit bust: 32-34-36-38 inches.
Lengths: 48-49-49-49 inches.
Women's Sizes: 32-34-36-38-40-42-44 bust.
Lengths: 48-49-49-49-49-49 inches.

State actual bust measure.

(A)

(B)

(C)

(D)

(E)

Smart Button Trim 4.98

Dainty White Lace Collar 2.98

Hand Smocked 2.98

(A) Buttons . . . covered to match the dress, running up and down those handsome sleeves and across the yoked neck! There's a pretty "window-box" collar, too, and three silvery flowers tucked under your chin. Shirring gives that soft bodice fullness. Slim, flared skirt!
Misses' Sizes: 14, 16, 18, 20. See size scale above. *State actual bust measure.*
31 L 3098 — Powder Blue.
31 L 3099 — Raspberry.
31 L 3100 — Navy Blue.
Shipping wt., 1 lb. 10 oz.

(B) Note how charmingly that double lace collar frames your face . . . and see what a slim young look that fitted peplum gives your hips! Covered buttons, puff sleeves, kick pleated skirt . . . what a lot of smartness! It's real Pebble Crepe of Celanese yarns.
Misses' Sizes: 14, 16, 18, 20. See size scale above. *State color and actual bust measure.*
31 L 3102 — Powder Blue, Navy or Medium Green.
Shipping wt., 1 lb. 6 oz.

(C) That high collar and pleated frill are of Rayon grosgrain ribbon. You'll like the trim fitted peplum too, and the flared skirt and below-the-elbow puff sleeves. Gorgeous colors in fine Pebble Crepe of Celanese yarns.
Misses' Sizes: 14, 16, 18, 20. See size scale above. *State actual bust measure.*
31 L 3105 — Navy with White.
31 L 3106 — Rose with White.
31 L 3107 — Powder Blue with Navy.
Shipping wt., 1 lb. 6 oz.

(D) 3.98 — Buttons, Bow and Belt in Contrast Color Crepe
You'll look as if you'd just stepped off Fifth Avenue in this dashing young Pebble Crepe of Celanese. With flared panel skirt, soft loose sleeves, generous hem.
Misses' Sizes: 14, 16, 18, 20. See size scale above. *State actual bust measure.*
31 L 3095 — Powder Blue with Navy.
31 L 3096 — Rose with Brown.
31 L 3097 — Navy with Powder Blue. $3.98
Shipping weight, 1 lb. 6 oz.

(E) 3.48 — Trim, Tucked Two-Piece Effect
Tiny stitched tucks trim the bodice, Snowy-white collar and cuffs and a metal fob lend a gay young air. Yoked action back! Real Rich Pebble Crepe of Celanese yarns.
Misses' Sizes: 14, 16, 18, 20. See size scale above. *State actual bust measure.*
31 L 3092 — Navy Blue.
31 L 3093 — Coral Rose.
31 L 3094 — Peacock Blue. $3.48
Shipping weight, 1 lb. 6 oz.

All dresses on this page are sent direct from New York to you, but you pay postage only from our nearest Mail Order House.

● SEARS-ROEBUCK PAGE 41

Smart moderns prefer dresses in Pebble Crepe woven of rich Celanese yarns. *Spring & Summer 1936*

$4.98

2-piece sports suit made of French finish All Rayon Crepe that looks like a corded, solid color silk. *Spring & Summer 1936*

Pebble Crepe Trimline dresses in slenderizing styles. *Spring & Summer 1936*

Beautiful long tunic slit hem dress is an autographed fashion that was worn in Hollywood by Loretta Young. *Spring & Summer 1935*

Water spotproof silk Canton crepe dresses in "Carefree" flattering styles. *Fall & Winter 1934*

Dresses have touches of white in silk crepe with organdy, 2-piece silk Matelasse, and eyelet Batiste jacket dress. *Spring & Summer 1935*

SWING ALONG the Avenue of Spring Fabric Fashions! All paths lead to Sears fairyland of 1935's smartest . . . rough weaves, big bold plaids, brilliant stripes, demure tiny designs. Beauteous silks, rayons, cottons, fleeciest woolens. You'll find, we're sure, the most complete collection in the world. And, best of all, everywhere you turn in this book, fabric prices are reduced to celebrate Sears big nation-wide "MAKE IT YOURSELF" contest. For inspiration, visions unbelievably lovely, see pages 144 to 153 and 164 to 177.

Slim, belted at the waist, a dress that is the new 1935 fashion.
Spring & Summer 1935

Dresses are all autographed fashions, worn in Hollywood by stars such as Ginger Rogers, Frances Dee, and Fay Wray. *Spring & Summer 1935*

Plain and print summer suit is tailored with a wide hem. Printed cotton jacket dress is cool, sheer and serviceable. *Spring & Summer 1935*

A variety of silk dresses for all occasions.
Spring & Summer 1935

Swagger, dressy, and tailored suit dress ensembles.
Spring & Summer 1935

SILK CREPE SUIT . . . .
EMBROIDERED EYELET
BATISTE BLOUSE . . . .

3-PIECE SUIT

...e of this season's newest
...les. A superior quality Silk
...nton Crepe (weighted)
...off by an exquisite Eyelet
...broidered Batiste blouse.
...ry flattering and femi-
...e. The blouse has a
...uthful Peter Pan collar
...l front frill edged with
...ated Batiste. Novelty
...ttons down front. Short
...gth sleeves. The skirt is cut on
...aight firm lines with box
...ats back and front. The
...ket is stunning, one of
... new finger tip lengths
...de with three-quarter
...gth sleeves—quite full,
...h a wide cuff. Jacket has
...at in back. Dark acces-
...ies to match the suit are
...art, dark gloves and
...es, and pocketbook, and
...dark silk or straw hat. Or
...ht accessories to match
...e blouse.

Sizes: 14-16-18-20 years.
Bust: 32-34-36-38 inches.
Lengths, about 49 in.
...H 8729—Navy
...th Lighter Blue. $6.98

Sent direct from New
...ork to you . . but you
...ay the postage only from
...ur nearest Mail Order
...ouse. See Page 12. Ship-
...ing weight, 2 lbs. 12 oz.

A "DRESS" SUIT—
SILK CREPE OR
BEMBERG SHEER

*Navy Blues—
Smarter than
Ever!*

AUTOGRAPHED FASHION
Worn in Hollywood by
Loretta Young
TRADE SUMMER FAVORITE STARED

Smart two piece suit with
double collar and cuffs of
two-color Permanent Finish
Organdy to harmonize with
the gorgeous print. Dress
has short sleeves. Your
choice of two beautiful, ex-
cellent quality fabrics.
Sizes: 14-16-18-20 years.
Bust: 32-34-36-38 inches.
Lengths about 49 inches.
State size and color.
Colors: Navy and White,
Lt. Wine and White, or
Black and White.

All Rayon
Bemberg Sheer . . $6.98
Glorious semi-sheer that
feels like softest silk and
wears better. Resists wrink-
les! Washable!
31 H 8732—Colors same as
above.

Printed Silk
Flat Crepe $6.98
A rich, fine weighted quality.
31 H 8735—Colors same as
above.
Sent direct from New
York . . . See Page 12. Ship-
ping weight, 1 lb. 6 oz. each.

JACKET Dresses
$6.98 Each

Page 23

LARGER SIZES COST

(E)
A Youthful
Style in Silk
Canton Crepe
$6.98

(F)
Slim-Fitting
Silk Crepe
$4.75

Silk Canton Crepe tunic dress has a detachable button-on bib. Silk Crepe dress has inverted tucks and buckles at the neck. *Spring & Summer 1935*

Silk Crepe suit has embroidered eyelet Batiste blouse is very flattering and feminine. An autographed fashion worn in Hollywood by Loretta Young has a double collar and cuffs of two-color organdy. *Spring & Summer 1935*

An autographed fashion worn in Hollywood by Adrienne Ames. This brand new style has a slightly flared silhouette, the dress is hand smocked in striking color contrast with rayon floss, has a high neck and gay button trim. Pleats in back and front, in rich Celanese Pebble Crepe fabric. *Fall & Winter 1935-1936*

Knits

With that "Hand-Knit" Look!

Nothing newer, smarter, more flattering!... Sears Knits are inexpensive but actually cost less than the yarn alone were you to buy it! Fine Quality— Gorgeous Colors!

Anne Williams

Both are Hand-Fashioned!

B All Wool Zephyr 6⁹⁸

C Finer Genuine Bouclé 7⁹⁵

A "Zippy" SPORTS STYLE

In All Wool $5⁹⁸

Descriptions on Opposite Page

E Slim! Genuine Bouclé 4⁹⁸

F Special! All Wool Worsted 3⁹⁸

G New! Shirt-maker 2⁹⁸

D The Popular "THREESOME" $3⁹⁸
COAT, BLOUSE and SKIRT

8 Sears

Fine quality knit ensembles in gorgeous fall colors to choose from. *Fall & Winter 1935-1936*

You'll be in

FASHION in NAVY BLUE

Of course these dresses also come in other new Fall Colors

Anne Williams

(A) Braid Is New **4⁷⁴**

(B) Collar Comes Off SPECIAL! **2⁹⁸**

(C) Princess Tunic Frock **4⁹⁸**

(D) Braid Applique on Net Sleeves **5⁹⁸**

WIDE HEMS FOR TALL WOMEN

Celanese Pe...

(A) Famous for w... bell sleeves ar... and when they contrasting braid th... A grand all-occasion... very low priced! Nev... ing at waistline. Misses' Sizes: 1... Women's Sizes: 3... measure. *State act...* Lengths, about 49 i... 31 K 2160—Navy an... 31 K 2161—Brown wi... 31 K 2162—Black an... Shipping weight, 1...

Fine Weighted...

(B) Just imagine ... dress like this ... cross-bar organ... collar for $2.98. A Ho... huge Pearl-like butto... Misses' Sizes: 14-... measure. *State size.* ... 31 K 2165—Navy with... 31 K 2166—Black with... 31 K 2167—Wine with... 31 K 2168—Purple wi... Shipping weight, 1...

Dresses shown on thi... pay...po...

,10

TALL WOMEN—These Dresses Have WIDE HEMS!

(F) Acetate or Silk Crepe **3⁹⁸**

(G) Paisley Print Trim **4⁹⁸**

(H) Silk Jacket Dress

NEVA-GAPE PLACKET
A New Aid To Smartness

• A Patented Feature Exclusive in Sears.
• Does Away With ...

Acetate or silk crepe dress, paisley print trim dress, and silk jacket dress. All dresses have Neva-Gape plackets. *Fall & Winter 1935-1936*

Celanese Crepe tunic, dresses, and three-piece suit. *Fall & Winter 1935-1936*

Celanese Pebble Crepe dress with big bell sleeves and embroidered contrasting braid. Weighted silk crepe dress with detachable cross-bar organdy and string lace collar. Celanese Pebble Crepe Princess Tunic frock has many buttons and pleated pockets. Celanese Ruff Crepe dress with full sleeves that run up into the shoulders. *Fall & Winter 1935-1936*

(E) Smart! Take-off

"Extra" Collar **49¢**

(F) Detachable F...

(G) Taffeta and Crepe

(H) Quilted Taffeta

Celanese Pebble Crepe dress with all-around corded collar with frog and cord trim. *Fall & Winter 1935-1936*

Blouse-back smocked dress made with quality Acetate Rayon Crepe in a smart rough weave. The dress features a high neckline and ¾ length sleeves. *Fall & Winter 1935-1936*

New
FASHIONS
at Sears
ECONOMY
PRICES!

All Garments on this page are shipped from New York but you pay postage only ... Mail Order House.

Dress suit in silk canton crepe has finger length jacket, wide collar revers, and box pleated skirt. Trimline dress with adjustable waist and a soft rayon vestee. *Fall & Winter 1935-1936*

Rayon and cotton ensemble has deep turn back cuffs and novelty pin. Tweedy cotton knit dress has high pointed collar and contrasting kerchief. Woven twilled plaid dress has contrasting Ascot tie and leather belt. Polka dot trim on rayon and cotton rough crepe with big bow and novelty sleeves. Two-piece sports outfit in woven cotton plaid with contrasting buttons and straight slim skirt. Print dress with lace edged white rayon and cotton collar has smart pleats in jabot and flattering new sleeves. *Fall & Winter 1935-1936*

Gowns

Glamorous "Best" Dresses
IN LOVELY PEBBLE CREPE

WOVEN OF RICH CELANESE YARNS

$4.98 **SHOWN ABOVE:** A one-piece shirtwaist dress made in very feminine fashion! Blouse part is SHEER SILK Chiffon—soft and cool looking with under bodice of rayon crepe. Full billowy sleeves, shirred at the top! Attached skirt is our best Pebble Crepe woven of fine Celanese yarns, preferred by most in silk.
Misses' Sizes: 14-16-18-20.
To Fit Bust: 32-34-36-38 in.
Lengths: 49-49-49-49 in.
State actual bust measure and color.
31 L 3210—Navy Blue, Powder Blue or Coral Rose.
Shipping weight, 1 lb. 6 oz.

$4.98 **SHOWN ABOVE:** You could shop for "ages" and not find as handsome an afternoon dress at this low price! It's a finer quality Pebble Crepe of rich Celanese yarns, lavishly trimmed with lacy hand drawn work across the front and back yoke, and down the full length of the sleeves! Collar ties in youthful becoming bow, with ends tipped with novelty pendants! Looks like a very expensive dress.
Misses' Sizes: 14-16-18-20.
To Fit Bust: 32-34-36-38 in.
Lengths: 53-54-54-54 in.
31 L 3215—Navy, Raspberry (Rosy Wine) or Powder Blue.
Shipping weight, 1 lb. 8 oz.

For 50 Years Brides Have Saved Money At Sears!

HAND DRAWN YOKE AND SLEEVES

"It's a gorgeous Party Frock—and in White is perfect for a Lovely Bride!"

$4.98 Down the wedding aisle — or whirling at a dance — this dress will be the center of all eyes! It's a glamorous affair made high at the throat and long at the ankle, with a flattering double collar, two self-material flowers, and soft shirred front yoke! Sleeves are full and long! Lines follow the figure! Our best Pebble Crepe! Woven of Celanese yarns!
State actual bust measure and color.
Women's Sizes: 34 to 44 in.
bust measure.
31 L 3225—White, Powder Blue or Coral Rose.
Shipping weight, 1 lb. 8 oz.

You'll Look Your Prettiest in This !

$2.98 It's an enchanting young fashion! It's made with a little high rolled collar and clips; double flare shoulder sleeves, soft shirring at the throat and V front. Fabric will stand a lot of partying and dancing in—a rich Pebble Crepe of fine Celanese yarns. See and feel the quality in actual sample on page 304. State size and color. Shpg. wt., 1 lb. 4 oz.
Misses' Sizes: 14-16-18-20.
To Fit Bust: 32-34-36-38 inches.
Lengths: 53-54-54-54 inches.
31 L 3220—National Blue, Aqua Blue, or Coral Rose.

The dresses on this page are sent direct from New York to you . . . but you pay postage only from our nearest Mail Order House.

● **SEARS-ROEBUCK** · **PAGE 47**

Two Pebble Crepe dresses with belted waists and long sleeves. Dress has double flare shoulder sleeves and soft shirring in rich Pebble Crepe. A gorgeous white party frock has a double collar and soft shirred front yoke. *Spring & Summer 1936*

ARE YOU TALLER THAN AVERAGE? these youthful dresses are designed for you! special long lengths, also in lengths for average height

New York Sponsors SOFT **WOOL ANGELENE** with **GLEAMING CREPE BACK SATIN** $4.98

A Smart Style

A Value Special

SILK FLAT CREPE $3.98

Enchanting— Glamorous!

TRANSPARENT VELVET $9.75

Glorious, gleaming Transparent Velvet—a superior quality with rich, deep rayon face and silk back! Dainty puffed sleeves of lace peek out under the gracious double tiered shoulders. Perfectly fitted hip yoke and full length panels to set off the graceful ankle flared skirt. Buckle-back bodice best of Velvet. The perfect "long" dress for those who like real instep length. Also special lengths for the tall woman.
State actual bust measure.
Women's Sizes: 34 to 44 in.
bust measure.
LONGER 56-IN. LENGTHS
31 F 7535—Black $9.75
REGULAR 53-IN. LENGTHS
31 F 7069—Black $9.75
Shipping weight, 1 lb. 8 oz.

The perfect combination for Fall—Wool and Crepe Black Silk Satin (weighted)! Angelene is a gorgeous downy napped fabric, more than one-half Wool with balance sturdy Cotton. It is knitted with the wool surface outside and with a smooth, non-irritating cotton on the back! Beautifully styled with bow closed neckline.
Women's and Misses' Sizes: 32 to 40 inches bust measure.
State bust measure and color.
LONGER 52-IN. LENGTHS
31 F 7545—Rust, French Almond (med. green) or Mulberry (wine).......$4.98
REGULAR 49-IN. LENGTHS
31 F 7072—Same colors as above.......$4.98
Shipping weight, 1 lb. 8 oz.

Stunning, wearable, tailored Silk Flat Crepe (weighted). Self material, detachable vestee is a lighter, blending tone. Neatly fitted panel skirt. This attractive dress belongs in every woman's wardrobe. It's a dress that goes everywhere smartly. One of the finest values we have ever offered.
Women's Sizes: 34 to 44 in. bust measure. State actual bust measure and color.
LONGER 51-IN. LENGTHS
31 F 7540—Medium Dark Brown, Mulberry (wine), Bright Navy Blue or Black.........$3.98
REGULAR 48-IN. LENGTHS
31 F 7075—Same colors as above.........$3.98
Shipping weight, 1 lb. 6 oz.

Send your order for above direct to New York. See Page 4.

Glorious transparent velvet dress has puffed sleeves with lace peeking out from double tiered shoulders. Wool and Crepe black silk satin dress is beautifully styled with a bow closed neckline. Tailored dress in silk flat Crepe has a detachable vestee and a neatly fitted panel skirt. *Fall & Winter 1934*

An autographed fashion worn in Hollywood by Ginger Rogers. Beruffled at the shoulders, slim and slinky about the hips and a swirling flare at the feet, this cotton Chiffon seersucker is cool enough for the hottest July nights. *Spring & Summer 1935*

Date or dance frocks in rayon taffeta or acetate crepe, transparent velvet or silk canton crepe, crepe back satin or acetate crepe, and lattice trim silk canton crepe. *Fall & Winter 1935-1936*

Beautiful evening gown with raglan sleeves, gleaming clips and buckle, in silk Canton Crepe, was worn in Hollywood by Loretta Young. Silk Crepe dress has a little standing collar in contrasting color. Sheer Organdy dress with large double tier collar and tiny cape sleeves. *Spring & Summer 1935*

Make a dramatic entrance in this evening dress and wrap, both made of shimmering transparent velvet. *Fall & Winter 1935-1936*

Hats

A selection of Anne Williams hats in fine, closely sewn Pedaline braid. *Spring & Summer 1936*

Sailor hats and turbans are made of imported hand-woven straw and lacy cellophane braid. *Spring & Summer 1934*

A variety of hats for the modern, up-to-date woman. *Fall & Winter 1934*

Big and beautiful flowered brim hats will add charm on any woman. *Spring & Summer 1935*

A selection of hats and turban for that reckless, jaunty look of 1935! *Spring & Summer 1935*

Bandeau hat with colorful flowers above. Cloche brim hat dips gaily beneath the bow. Cellophane turban has a veil and flower on it's peaked top. Hand woven Peanit straw hat with velvet ribbon trimming. *Spring & Summer 1935*

The Bouquet Beret is inspired by the new motion picture "Man of Aran" and is made of fine pedaline straw braid. Ciré ribbons and two matching gardenias adorn this beret. *Spring & Summer 1935*

Every one of these hats are flattering and easy to wear. *Spring & Summer 1935*

An autographed fashion worn in Hollywood by Adrienne Ames. Felt hat has all
wool body with a brim that turns down in
front and up in back. *Fall & Winter 1935-
1936*

These felt hats are all new
for this fall and come in
such interesting fashions.
Fall & Winter 1935-1936

1^{59} EACH

All wool body felt with cord-topped dagger. All woold body hat with peaked crown and a dashing feather. *Fall & Winter 1935-1936*

Each a Leading FALL FASHION! IN ALL WOOL FELT FABRIC! 59¢ EACH

Headsize? — A tape measure will tell! 35

All wool felt fabric hats. *Fall & Winter 1935-1936*

All wool body felt hat with rayon satin ribbon. Turban is wool crepe with tucked banding twirled up at side with a smart gilt buckle. *Fall & Winter 1935-1936*

Lingerie

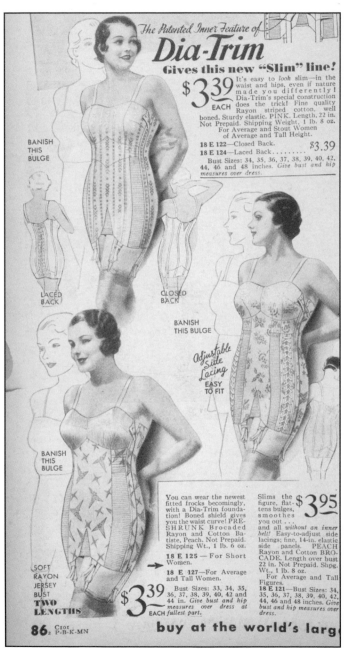

Pure silk chiffons have picot tops, French heels, seamless feet, and double sandal soles. *Spring & Summer 1934*

Dia-Trim gives support and flattens the bulges in the diaphragm area to allow confidence in wearing silhouette dresses. *Spring & Summer 1934*

Lastex back step in style, satin Lastex pantie girdle, Lastex-batiste with talon closing, Softie power Lastex, and Lastex back with talon zip sets a good foundation for smart spring outfits. *Spring & Summer 1936*

Full silk or satin slips are luxurious under your loveliest frocks. *Spring & Summer 1936*

Royal Purple "Desirable" stockings. *Spring & Summer 1936*

Charmodes are the beauty secret of splendid figures! *Fall & Winter 1934*

A selection of wool weight slips for warmth under your finest dresses. *Fall & Winter 1934*

"Purple" silk hosiery in sheer chiffon, service chiffon, and service weight. *Fall & Winter 1934*

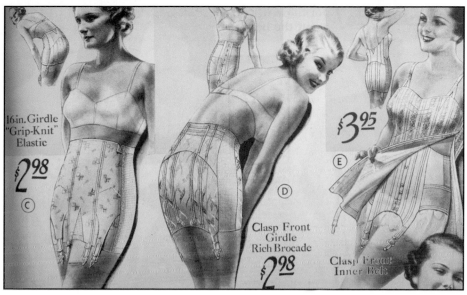

A variety of "Nu-Back" girdles with the famous patented sliding back feature. *Spring & Summer 1935*

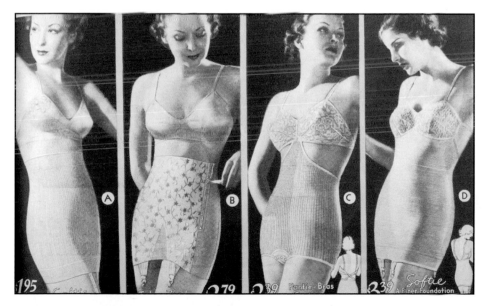

Keep that youthful figure with Sears Lastex girdles that feature 2-way stretch for comfort. *Spring & Summer 1935*

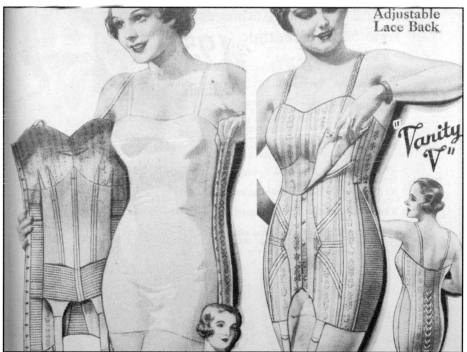

Elastic and boning inner shield flattens tummy and diaphragm. "Vanity V" girdle clasps in the front and brassiere hooks on the side. *Spring & Summer 1935*

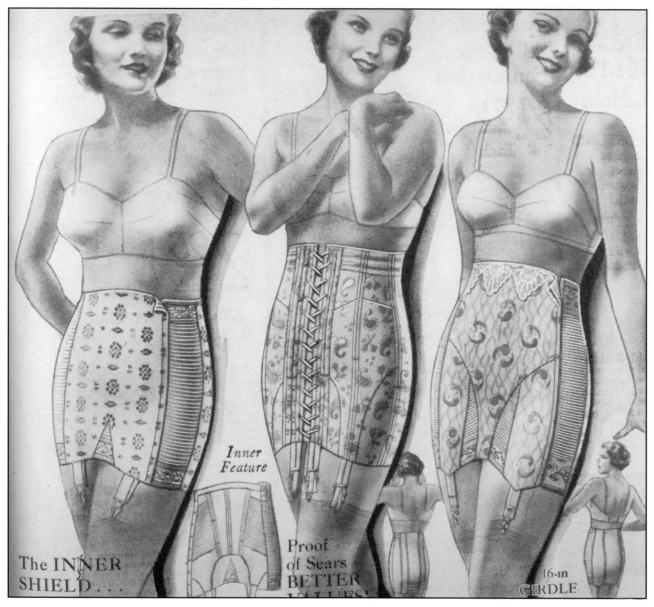

The INNER
SHIELD...

*Inner
Feature*

Proof
of Sears
BETTER
VALUES!

16-in
GIRDLE

Girdles to fit your every need in three different lengths. *Spring & Summer 1935*

Knit rayon vest and bloomers in two different styles. *Spring & Summer 1935*

Lowest
Prices
For
Good Quality
KNIT RAYON

19c

EACH

CHOICE
OF ANY
OF THESE
TAILORED
UNDIES

They're Cut to Fit

Stand
hard wear
and washing

52

A variety of lingerie, pajamas, and sweaters of 1935. *Spring & Summer 1935*

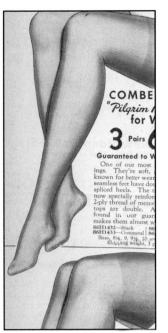

"Pilgrim Positive-Wear" are guaranteed to wear for 3 months in 2-ply thread of mercerized cotton. *Spring & Summer 1935*

Pure silk, rayon and silk, and dull rayon stockings. *Spring & Summer 1935*

Ribbed stockings with stretchy tops for comfort. *Spring & Summer 1935*

"Lady Pilgrim" cotton union suits in closed seat with wide knee, open seat with wide knee, or open seat with tight knee styles. *Spring & Summer 1935*

Assorted selection of slips, pajamas, and gowns. *Fall & Winter 1935-1936*

Sears Cotton Slips

Knit-to-fit and retain their shape

Also Regular Sizes

Also Stout Sizes

Knit slips in wool and cotton fabrics. *Fall & Winter 1935-1936*

Brassieres in elastic knit cotton, rayon and cotton brocade, and Alencon type lace fabrics. *Fall & Winter 1935-1936*

A

B

Stockings in rayon over wool and cotton, wool and silk, and rayon outside with wool inside. *Fall & Winter 1935-1936*

Shoes

Stylish shoes that go with the new fashions in oxfords and kid styles.
Spring & Summer 1934

A selection of shoes for the young college girl. *Spring & Summer 1934*

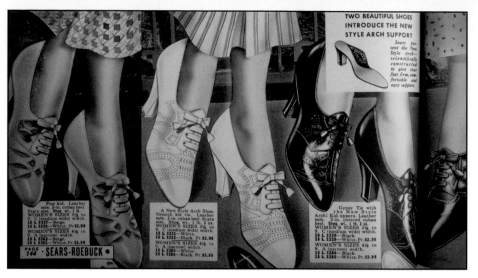

Leather sole tie shoes in 3 lovely styles. *Spring & Summer 1936*

Sandals in many different styles for the modern woman. *Spring & Summer 1936*

Autographed fashion worn in Hollywood by Mary Brian. Graceful sandal with narrow T-strap and spike heel. In white or black kid leather. *Spring & Summer 1935*

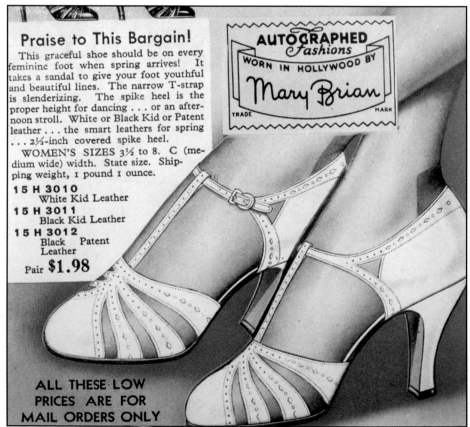

Shoes in smart Colonial styles, oxfords, pumps, and moccasins. *Fall & Winter 1934*

Autographed fashion worn in Hollywood by Frances Dee. Kiltie has boldly slashed tounges, buckle straps across the instep, and airy perforations. *Spring & Summer 1935*

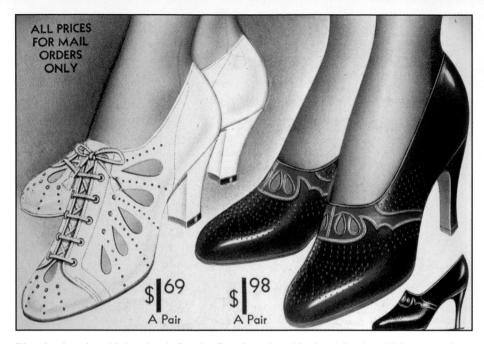

$1⁶⁹ A Pair

$1⁹⁸ A Pair

Bicycle shoe has higher heels for the first time, in white buck leather. Kid pump with spike heel has perforations in the trim in brown or black. *Spring & Summer 1935*

$2⁵⁹ A Pair
Black

$1⁹⁸ A Pair
Blue

Graceful Cut Gives It Style
A handsome tongueless 4-eyelet tie for sedate

Dark Blue or Beige
Spring comes in with a flurry of navy blue

Autographed fashion worn in Hollywood by Joan Marsh, this white cut-out has 3-eyelet tongue in fine grained leather. Handsome tongueless 4-eyelet tie has tiny cut-outs and graceful rows of stitching in brown and black colors. Navy blue or beige kid oxford is tailored with beautiful stitching and is perforated. *Spring & Summer 1935*

Fresh from Hollywood's FASHION *Parade*

We Prophesy White and Brown for Sports
1935—another brown and white year! This white elk grained leather oxford has a brown shawl tongue . . . swagger as can be. Popular rubber sport sole. Flexible stitchdown construction. 1¾-inch walking heel; rubber top lift.
WOMEN'S SIZES 2½ to 8. C (medium wide) width.

The Price That Set the Girls Talking—About Sears Values
Low heels took Hollywood by storm—and young girls will be proud to wear these. Sporty style with fringe effect and neat buckle strap across the instep. Perforated. Patent leather is a favorite in this style. 1¼-inch walking heel; rubber top lift. Long wearing leather sole.
WOMEN'S SIZES 2½ to 8. C (medium wide) width.

$1⁹⁸ A Pair

White elk grained leather oxford sports shoe has a brown shawl tongue and rubber sole. Autographed fashion worn in Hollywood by Ginger Rogers has low heels in a sporty style with fringe effect and buckle strap. *Spring & Summer 1935*

For Riding Clothes See Page 60

Riding boots for the equestrienne in pull-on or lace-up styles. *Spring & Summer 1935*

Correct Shoes Prevent Foot Ills

—Handsome 4-Eyelet tie; soft, smooth, black durable, genuine kidskin.
—Cushion insoles and wrinkleless quarter linings. —High quality leather soles.
Fashionable comfort shoe! 1⅞-inch military heels; rubber top lifts.
WOMEN'S SIZES 3½ to 8; also 9. D (wide) width. State size. Shipping weight, 1 pound 7 ounces.
15 H 3556—Pair............$1.49

$1.49 A Pair

Trim Black Kidskin

—Nightingale comfort features.
—Fine quality genuine kidskin.
—High quality leather soles.
Shoes you feel "at home" in. No pressure anywhere. 1-inch heels with rubber top lifts that absorb shock.
WOMEN'S SIZES 2½ to 8; also 9. D (wide) width. State size. Shipping weight, 1 pound 7 ounces.
15 H 3414—Pair............$1.39

$1.39

Black leather shoes provide comfort while walking with low heels and rubber top lifts to absorb shock. *Spring & Summer 1935*

Soft black suede print leather seen only in the most exclusive shoes. Trimmed in shiny black patent leather. Leather sole. 1¾-inch cuban heel.
WOMEN'S SIZES 3½ to 8. C (medium wide) width. State size. Shipping weight, 1 pound 1 ounce.
15 K 3082—Pair..$1.59

Our buyers went in search of Fashion's latest whim! And they found Basquette—the smart embossed leather—designed to look like basket-weave. A modern adaptation of the Alpine shoe with its famous flaring tongue. Smooth leather trim. Leather sole. 1¾-inch cuban heel.
WOMEN'S SIZES 3½ to 8. C (medium wide) width. State size. Shipping wt., 1 pound 1 ounce.
15 K 3083—Brown.
15 K 3084—Black.
$1.59 Pair

Autographed fashion, worn in Hollywood by Virginia Oherrill, shoes in soft black suede print leather and Basquette basket-weave leather. *Fall & Winter 1935-1936*

LIGHT DRESSY
Snap-on

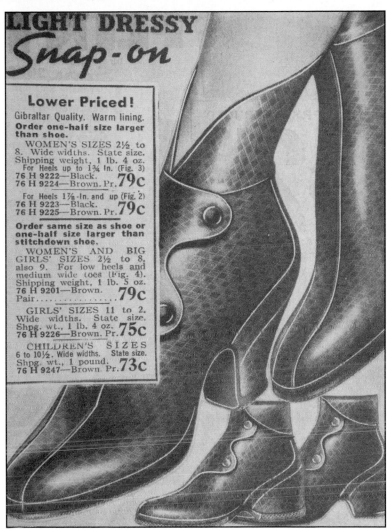

Lower Priced!

Gibraltar Quality. Warm lining.
Order one-half size larger than shoe.
WOMEN'S SIZES 2½ to 8. Wide widths. State size. Shipping weight, 1 lb. 4 oz.
For Heels up to 1¾ in. (Fig. 3)
76 H 9222—Black.
76 H 9224—Brown. Pr. 79c

For Heels 1⅞-in. and up (Fig. 2)
76 H 9223—Black.
76 H 9225—Brown. Pr. 79c

Order same size as shoe or one-half size larger than stitchdown shoe.
WOMEN'S AND BIG GIRLS' SIZES 2½ to 8, also 9. For low heels and medium wide toes (Fig. 4).
Shipping weight, 1 lb. 5 oz.
76 H 9201—Brown. Pair.... 79c

GIRLS' SIZES 11 to 2. Wide widths. State size. Shpg. wt., 1 lb. 4 oz.
76 H 9226—Brown. Pr. 75c

CHILDREN'S SIZES 6 to 10½. Wide widths. State size. Shpg. wt., 1 pound.
76 H 9247—Brown. Pr. 73c

Gibraltar quality lined snap-on boots. *Spring & Summer 1935*

Tree Bark—still one of the smartest leathers you can buy for autumn. A beautiful oxford! Leather sole. 2½-inch covered continental heel. **WOMEN'S SIZES** 3½ to 8. C (medium wide) width. State size. Shpg. wt., 1 lb. 3 oz. **15 K 3045**–Black with Patent Leather **15 K 3044**–Camel Color with Brown. Pair.... **$1⁹⁸**

163

Tree bark leather oxford is an autographed fashion worn in Hollywood by Marion Nixon. *Fall & Winter 1935-1936*

Black printed suede leather pump is a Hollywood fashion worn by Sally Eilers. *Fall & Winter 1935-1936*

167

Autographed fashion worn in Hollywood by Adrienne Ames, this kid has stitching in smart swirls and the new gypsy tie. *Fall & Winter 1935-1936*

Fine grained leather boots have Goodyear welt and leather heel and sole. *Fall & Winter 1935-1936*

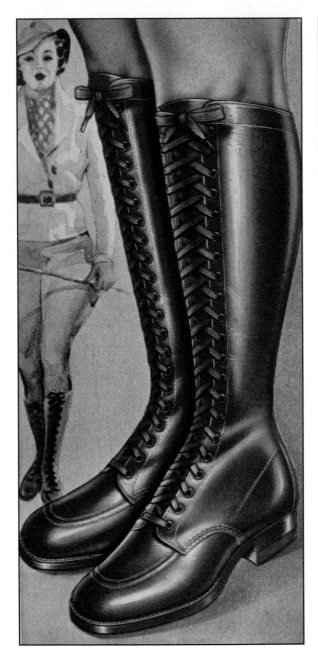

Laced chrome tanned brown leather boots have Goodyear welt construction. *Fall & Winter 1935-1936*

Snap-on galoshes with stand-up cuff have warm fleece lining. *Fall & Winter 1935-1936*

Gibraltar fur top boots in satin finish rubber. Jiffy galoshes have slide fastener in black or brown rubber. Satin finish evening boots with soft, black genuine coney fur tops. *Fall & Winter 1935-1936*

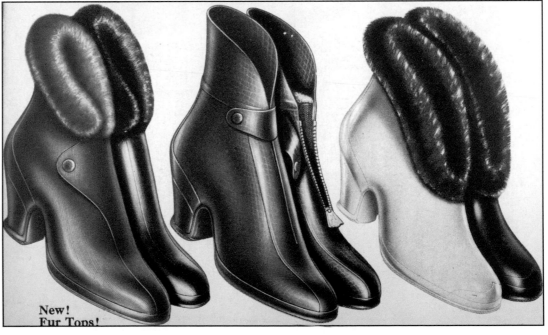

Accessories

$1.39 (F) Shining brilliant metal cloth scarf. Goes with all colors! Soft, supple; smooth to the touch! Lined with weighted silk Crepe. Unusual Value.
18 K 3406 — Gold or Silver color. State color. Size, 38½x9¼ in. Shipping weight, 7 ounces.

(G) Quilted Rayon Taffeta! The 65c smartest neckwear idea in years! Soft, light and flat. Ties neatly.
18 K 3407 — Color: White. Length, 39½ in. Width at ends, 8½ in. Shipping weight, 6 ounces.

79c (H) Light, sheer, wool, interwoven with gold metal threads! A really fine triangle that you see in the best shops at much higher prices! Self fringed edge.
18 K 3414 — Size, 32x21x14 in. Colors: Chili (medium) Brown, Green, Tuscan Wine, Violet, Rust, Navy Blue. State color. Shipping weight, 4 ounces.

(J) Soft, heavy weighted silk crepe! 25c In the smart triangle style! With a neatly embroidered monogram effect. Self fringed.
18 K 3408 — Size, 27x17 in. Colors: White, Red, Chili Brown, Navy Blue, Medium Green. State color. Shipping wt., 4 oz.

Metal Cloth!

Quilted

Metal Thread Wool

Silk Crepe Triangle

Scotch Plaid

85c (K) Luxurious Zephyr Wool. Extra size, 50x 10½ inches.
18 K 3410 — Bright plaids. Combination colors of Tan and Brown, Red and Navy, Yellow and Black, Copen and Navy, White and Black. State color. Shipping weight, 7 ounces.
All Wool Scarf. Not illustrated similar to (K). Size, 43x9 in.
18 K 3411 — Predominating colors: Red, Brown Royal Blue, Black or White. State color. Shpg. wt., 6 oz .. 39c

(L) Roman Striped Scarf. Size, 25c 7x51 inches.
18 K 3412 — Dominant colors: Navy, Red, Brown or Black with White. State color. Shipping weight, 4 ounces.
Windsor Scarf (not illustrated). Size, 47x7¼ inches.
18 K 3413 — Solid colors: Scarlet, Navy, Black or White. State color. Shipping weight, 4 ounces............ 23c

25c (M) Use as an ascot, too. 8½x56 in.
18 K 3415 Predominating colors: Brown, Blue or Red. State color. Shipping wt., 4 oz.

(N) Acetate Crepe. 25c Size, 27x 20½ inches.
18 K 3409 — Colors: White, Rust, Royal Blue, Gold. State color. Shipping weight, 4 ounces.

Plaid Rayon Taffeta

Silk-Striped or Plain

Hand Knotted

A variety of scarves to brighten up any wardrobe. *Fall & Winter 1935-1936*

Fine Botany Woolen coats for misses and juniors. One has a corded taffeta collar, the other frog and button trim. *Spring & Summer 1936*

Junior and misses coats in checks, tweed, plaid, and reefer styles. *Spring & Summer 1936*

Collegiate Fashions

JUNIOR SIZE SCALE	MISSES' SIZE SCALE
Sizes: 13-15-17-19	Sizes: 14-16-18-20
To fit bust: 31-33-35-37 in.	To fit bust: 32-34-36-38 in.
Lengths: 46-47-48-49 in.	Lengths: 48-49-49-49 in.

Choice of Two Fabrics $4.98 UP

Novelty Tweed $5.98

...thing checks (they're smart this season!) or rich Tan Polo type coat— Both are about half Wool, with ...ton and Rayon added for greater ...ngth and beauty. Belted back! ...ranteed sateen lined! *State color ... size* . . . see size scale above.
NOVELTY CHECK COATING
Colors: Gray or Lt. Brown Checks.
... 6455—Junior Sizes.
... 6155—Misses' Sizes . . . $4.98
TAN POLO COAT
... 6460—Junior Sizes.
... 6160—Misses' Sizes . . . $5.98
...hipping weight, 3 lbs. 4 oz. each.

Full-cut and very swagger—the sort of coat you can wear over everything from sports clothes to your dressiest print! The lovely "Window-Pane" tweed is about two-thirds Wool and Silk Noil, balance fine Rayon and Cotton to give richness and strength. The draped petal collar is a new Paris idea and you'll adore the big buttons. Full Rayon and Cotton lined.
Colors: Medium Green, Medium Blue, or Medium Tan. *State size and color*; see size scale above. Lgths. 45 ins.
17 L 6465—Junior Sizes.
17 L 6165—Misses' Sizes . . . $5.98
Shipping weight, 3 lbs. 8 oz.

$6.98 UP

$5.98

Plaids! Big, Bold, Beautiful!
IN THE NEW STROLLER LENGTH SWAGGER with the jaunty, bias cut fishtail back! A Dorothy Wilson autographed fashion. Of soft fine plaid that's half Wool, half Rich Rayon. Double collar, big novelty buttons! Rayon and cotton lining. Shpg. wt., 2 lbs. 6 oz.
Colors: Lt. Brown Ombre Plaid or Med. Blue Ombre Plaid. *State color and actual bust measure* . . . see size scale above.
17 L 6480—Junior Sizes.
17 L 6180—Misses' Sizes $5.98

◄IN TWO GORGEOUS SPRING FABRICS
Rich, luxurious ALL WOOL Botany Worsted, or fine quality Crepe Coating, about nine-tenths Wool with Rayon and Cotton added for longer wear. Reefer style, with the new yoke pleated back! Metal fob and buttons! *State actual bust measure* . . . see size scale above for lengths. Shps. wt., 3 lbs.
Colors: Navy Blue.
ALL WOOL BOTANY WORSTED
Silk Crepe Weighted Lining
17 L 6475—Junior Sizes.
17 L 6175—Misses' Sizes $9.98
WOOL CREPE COATING
Lustrous Rayon Lining
17 L 6470—Junior Sizes.
17 L 6170—Misses' Sizes $6.98

● SEARS-ROEBUCK ● PAGE 25

All coats on this page sent direct from New York to you . . . but you pay postage only from our nearest Mail Order House.

Your Choice $10.95 Each

Both in

All wool jacket with zip closing, tweed jacket in herringbone weave, peasant linen checked jacket, and tuxedo-type jacket in velveteen. *Spring & Summer 1936*

Autographed Fashion fine polo coat worn in Hollywood by Anita Louise. All wool gay plaid coat. Fancy rough knobby tweed coat. All wool tree bark Crepe coat with snappy cape. *Spring & Summer 1935*

JUNIOR MISS
SIZES 13 TO 19

Fringe Scarf Coat

E

F
New Wide Belt

D
White Waffle Coating
$2⁹⁵

Crepolaine Coating

Novelty Check Tweed

$6⁹⁸ Each

Expensive Looking—
but look at Sears Low Prices!

Our Finest Tree Bark

Silk Lined
$8⁹⁸

Choice of Novelty Tweed or All Wool Crepe

Short and Snappy
$1⁸⁹

D WHITE COTTON WAFFLE cloth makes a love of a summer coat! Swank young model made of a strong supple quality that gives to the figure without any unbecoming sag. White buttons and artificial leather belt. Unlined.
Junior Miss Sizes: 13-15-17-19 years.
Bust Measures: 31-33-35-37 inches. *State bust.*
Lengths, about 46 inches.
17 H 9430—White............ $2.95
Shipping weight, 3 lbs. 12 oz.

E STITCHING IS SMARTER than ever! Especially on this slim tailored dress coat. Fine quality Crepolaine Coating (70% Wool, balance Rayon and Cotton for richness and durability). Lined with Rayon and Cotton.
Junior Miss Sizes: 13-15-17-19 years.
Bust Measures: 31-33-35-37 inches. *State bust.*
Lengths, about 47 inches.
17 H 9435—Light Navy Blue.
17 H 9436—Medium Tan...... $6.98
Shipping weight, 2 lbs. 12 oz.

F SWAGGER THROUGH SPRING with this jaunty sports coat. Novelty Check Coating is about half Wool and Silk Noil strengthened with Rayon and Cotton. Lining of Rayon and Cotton. *State bust measure.*
Junior Miss Sizes: 13-15-17-19 years.
Bust Measures: 31-33-35-37 inches.
Lengths, about 47 inches.
17 H 9440—Gold and Blue Check.
17 H 9441—Blue and Gray Check.
17 H 9442—Green and Gray Check............ $6.98
Shipping weight, 3 lbs. 6 oz.

IT'S GAY AND DASHING LOOKING! MADE WITH nice big comfy pockets and a pert Ascot tie that can be worn several ways. Just the kind of a coat to bring a modern maiden's spirits up to where they should be—on top of the world! The belt pulls you in slimly at the waist, and gives a sporty air. Collar has loads of stitching. Fabric is that soft "tweedy" Tree Bark Coating, over one-half wool, and balance Rayon. Excellent quality Silk Crepe (weighted) lining. It's low priced, too. You'll adore it! Lengths, about 47 inches.
Junior Sizes: 13-15-17-19 years.
Bust Measures: 31-33-35-37. *State bust measure.*

Half-Wool Novelty Tree Bark Tweed
17 H 9445—Light Green.
17 H 9446—Medium Tan.
17 H 9447—Medium Blue............ $8.98

Coats for misses in white waffle, Crepolaine, novelty checked tweed, and tree bark materials. *Spring & Summer 1935*

Glossy as Real Fur! A DEEP RAYON and Cotton Pile fabric that reproduces the exquisite beauty of genuine Broadtail fur. Rayon and cotton lined.
Stout Sizes: 37, 39, 41, 43, 45 and 47 in. bust measure. *State bust measure.*
17 H 9475—Rich Black.
17 H 9476—Medium Brown.
17 H 9477—Medium Gray.......... $4⁴⁵
Sent direct from New York to you... See Page 12.
Shipping weight, 2 lbs. 4 oz.

FUR FABRICS
that Simulate Broadtail
Glorify These
Youthful Jackets

Glossy rayon and cotton pile jacket looks like genuine Broadtail fur. Jacket with high crushed collar in rayon and cotton fabric. *Spring & Summer 1935*

Genuine Swavel cloth jacket is double breasted with center pleat for roominess. Corduroy jacket has a pleated back and belted front. *Spring & Summer 1935*

Genuine Swavel
$1⁹⁸

Corduroy is Smart!
$2⁹⁸

New Action Back

Pleat Panel Back

All wool fleece set in plaid and solid colors. All wool jacket and pants set. All wool Chinchilla coat with cotton plaid lining. *Fall & Winter 1935-1936*

Broadtail fur fabric jacket looks like real fur. *Fall & Winter 1935-1936*

Rubberized cotton tweed coat and hat. Waterproof cotton Suede-Tex coat with matching beret. *Fall & Winter 1935-1936*

Pig grain jacket is Hollywood's latest fashion. Cossack jacket in fine glove leather. Autographed fashion Cossack jacket worn in Hollywood by Dorothy Wilson is fine suede leather. *Fall & Winter 1935-1936*

Dresses

Modern New York fashions for the junior miss in dotted Swiss, printed silk crepe, silk flat crepe, and all silk Canton crepe fabrics. *Spring & Summer 1934*

This jacket frock is the hit of New York with smart light top and a sunburst of tucks. Dorothy Wilson's pet suit has wide rever jacket with cuffs of white Coney fur. *Spring & Summer 1936*

High Necklines are Favorites in the Collegiate Shop

Ⓐ FINE SILK CREPE **3**⁸⁸
"Classroom Chic" RAYON TAFFETA TRIM

Ⓑ Flower Splashed "Allure" **$2.98**

"Swel-elegant" with a rustly TAFFETA COLLAR that's detachable **$3.98** Ⓒ

Ⓓ For a change wear this String Lace Jabot Collar **49¢**

Ⓔ "Special Date" You'll look your loveliest in gleaming TRANSPARENT VELVET **$8**⁷⁵

Ⓕ You'll be a Shining Star in "Class Party" **$5**⁹⁸
IT'S IN THE WARDROBE OF THIS MOVIE STAR
See the Label!
AUTOGRAPHED Fashions WORN IN HOLLYWOOD BY Lilian Bond

Dresses for the junior miss in "Classroom Chic," "Allure," "Swel-elegant," "Special Date," and "Class Party" styles. *Fall & Winter 1934*

Fashions that "click" on every Campus are the fashions shown in Sears Collegiate Shop

Ⓓ "Run-about" A dashing THREE-PIECE WOOL **$5**⁹⁵

Ⓔ "Saucy" Shows how a big Taffeta Bow can flatter! TWO-PIECE WOOL **$3**⁹⁸

Ⓒ "Sport Pair" with PLAID SLIP-OVER **$2**⁶⁵ and Swagger VELVETEEN SKIRT **$2**⁹⁸
Autographed And worn by a star
Be Proud of this Label
AUTOGRAPHED Fashions WORN IN HOLLYWOOD BY Joan Bennett

Ⓐ "Top-Notch" TWO-PIECE KNIT **$1**⁹⁸

Ⓑ "Frills" Taffeta TRIM **$3**

Smart young moderns wear "Co-ed's"

From the Sears Collegiate Shop, "Run-about," "Saucy," "Sport Pair (worn in Hollywood by Joan Bennett)," "Top-Notch," and "Frills" styled dresses for the junior miss. *Fall & Winter 1934*

73

Pretty one- and two-piece dresses and jumpers for the junior miss in all the favorite fashions. *Spring & Summer 1935*

"Bunny Ear" frock in white cotton pique with bright red buttons and self belt. Cotton crop dress has cap sleeves and smart patch pockets. Cotton pique dress with graceful collar and tie. *Spring & Summer 1935*

Acetate rayon crepe Bolero dress with contrasting colors. Acetate rayon crepe dress has shirred shoulders and neckline with contrasting colors. *Fall & Winter 1935-1936*

Dresses for the young miss in one- and two-piece styles. *Spring & Summer 1935*

Pique Jumper
with Organdy
Blouse
$1.49

Eyelet
Batiste
$1.69

A Gay
Plaid
75¢

Crisp
Organdy
$1.19

Cool
Batiste
$1.19

A Kerchief
for Dash
70¢

Three Lovely 8 to 14 Fashions

P NEW SQUARE Ruffled Neckline of Permanent Finish Organdy. Double ruffling forms cap sleeves. Cool sheer frock in Eyelet Embroidered Cotton Batiste. Organdy mult. Sizes: 8 to 14 yrs. State size. 27 H 6408—Copen Blue. 27 H 6461—Med. $1.69

R A REAL VALUE for a Real Girl! Bright spring Plaid in sturdy printed Washfast Percale. Novelty-edged Cotton Linene trim. Peppy young skirt is smartly flounced and pleated. State age size. Sizes: 8 to 14 years. 27 H 6405—Fancy Plaid. 75¢

S LARGE SQUARE Cape Collar with ruffled edge and dainty flower makes this the newest and prettiest Organdy frock anywhere. Soft full skirt has a deep flounce. Sizes: 8 to 14 years. 27 H 6418—Lt. Blue. 27 H 6411—Maize. 27 H 6405—White. $1.19

A
"Nautical"
Fashion
98¢

Printed
Broadcloth
98¢

Organdy
and Eyelets
$1.98

Page 67

June O'Day
modes for the
JUNIOR MISS
Sizes 13 to 19 Years

E
Taffeta
Trims It!
$3.75

F
Take-off
Collar
$2.98

H
Shirred
Tunic
$3.98

G
Alluringly
Lovely Velvet
$7.98

Here's
GLAMOUR
and
STYLE!

Genuine
Celanese
Ruff Crepe

AN AUTOGRAPHED FASHION
Worn in Hollywood by
Dorothy Wilson

$5.95

No wonder Hollywood stars are called smart! Just look at this two-piece . . a stunning Dorothy Wilson model in new Ruff Celanese Crepe. You will love the luxurious feel of this expensive looking material. It is wrinkle resistant, and very rich as to color, and much preferred by many over silk. Dress has monogrammed contrasted top with high roll collar. Six big buttons on pleated skirt. Take off the jaunty jacket and you have a perfectly gorgeous dress. A bargain at $5.95.

E Top Value! Extra wide revers—perky bow—gilet-effect; all made of crisp Rayon Taffeta Crepe—the fabric preferred for style and rich colors. Buttons down front of pleated skirt.
Sizes: 13-15-17-19 years.
Bust: 31-33-35-37 inches. State size.
31 K 2740—Navy Blue.
31 K 2741—Dark Blue. $3.75

G New York's Smartest "Dress up" dress! New high neck and long full sleeves! Rich gleaming Rayon-faced Transparent Velvet with Silk Back. Silver imitation leather belt and bow. Brilliant buttons. You'll be the hit of the party!
Sizes: 13-15-17-19 years.
Bust: 31-33-35-37 inches.
Lengths, about 54 inches. State size.
31 K 2725—Black.
31 K 2726—French Violet (Purple).
31 K 2727—Rich Wine $7.98

"Junt O'Day" modes for the junior miss are both glamorous and stylish. *Fall & Winter 1935-1936*

Belted cotton dresses in a wide selection of styles. *Spring & Summer 1935*

Here are some of the exciting styles of the mid-thirties. Shirtmakers, Action Backs, New Necklines. Young-Gay-Packed full of style. *Fall & Winter 1935-1936*

Velveteen blouse and plaid tweed skirt. Silk flat crepe dress with peplum front gives a two-piece effect. *Fall & Winter 1935-1936*

Cotton print top and skirt is solid color cotton broadcloth. Rayon and cotton print dress has ruffle collar with contrasting bow. 2-piece suit in warm tweed. Print percale dress has pleated all-around skirt flounce. Sailor dress in sturdy cotton crepe. *Fall & Winter 1935-1936*

About half wool Flannel, balance cotton yarns, balanced skirt. Full length blouse of washfast cotton print. Quality at a low price!

27 K 4260—Navy with Red Print.

27 K 4261—Brown with Maize Print. Shipping wt., 1 lb. 3 oz.

Both in Sizes: 8, 10, 12 and 14 years. State age-size.

SIZE SCALE

Sizes: 8-10-12-14 yrs.
Chest: 27-29-31-33 in.
L'gth: 29-32-35-39 in.

In two materials! Ruffle trimmed cape collar, flounced skirt.

Colors: Medium Blue or Medium Rose. State color.

Silk Crepe $2.49
27 K 4264

Rayon and Cotton Crepe $1.39
27 K 4266 Shpg. wt., 1 lb. ea.

Two-Piece Effect 69¢

Good quality Cotton print top with skirt of solid color Cotton Broadcloth. Skirt has front pleats. A lovely young style—smart enough to go anywhere. A value feature.
Sizes: 8, 10, 12 and 14 years. State age-size.

27 K 4276—Fancy Print with Navy Blue Skirt. Shipping wt., 12 oz.

See Pages 75, 80 and 81 for other Girls' Dresses.

Rayon and Cotton Print $1.00

Rayon for dress-up! You know how pretty it is and how well it wears! Soft ruffle collar with contrasting bow. Puffed sleeves; skirt is smartly flared.
Sizes: 8, 10, 12 and 14 years. State age-size.

27 K 4280—Wine.
27 K 4281—Navy. Shipping wt., 10 oz.

WONDER VALUE

Action-Back 2-Piece Suit $2.98

Jacket and skirt are a warm tweed; half wool, balance silk noile. Attached blouse is washfast cotton print—with cap sleeves and Peter Pan collar.
Sizes: 8, 10, 12, 14 and 16 years. State age-size.

27 K 4284—Navy.
27 K 4285—Brown. Shipping wt., 2 lbs.

Woven plaid 2-piece suit with cotton serge skirt. Plaid cotton crepe dress. Angorette knit dress in shirtmaker style. Kerchief frock in cotton pongette. Percale dress with fagotted white cotton pique trim. *Fall & Winter 1935-1936*

2-PIECE OUTFIT $1.98

Woven Plaid Suiting with Cotton Serge Skirt

Both fabrics noted for their long wear and good looks. Wide smart revers and wooden buttons on the rich plaid jacket! It has the new yoke back, too! Solid color skirt has all-round pleated flounce. State bust measure.
Misses' Sizes: 14 to 20 to fit 32 to 38 in. bust measure.

27 K 3812—Red and Navy Blue. Shipping weight, 1 lb. 8 oz.

.70

$1.49 Zip Closed

In Plaid Cotton Crepe Suiting, with shirred front and back. Wooly Pompon. State bust measure.
Sizes: 14 to 20 years to fit 32 to 38 in. bust.

27 K 3792—Red and Blue.
27 K 3793—Brown and Yellow. Shipping wt., 1 lb. 2 oz.

$1.98 Angorette New Knit

Smart shirtmaker style. A warm knit with a silvery gleam! Cotton and Rayon combined with Wool Mohair! Sizes: 32 to 44 in. bust. State size.

27 K 3800—Concord Blue.
27 K 3801—Wine. Shipping wt., 1 lb. 12 oz.

Lustrous Cotton 98¢

The sport 'kerchief frock! In washfast cotton Pongette! A striking print! Pleated sport sleeves! Skirt has smart pleats.
Sizes: 13 to 19 years. State size.

27 K 3816—Navy Blue and Red. Shpg. wt., 12 oz.

27 K 3808—Wine.
27 K 3809—Navy Blue.
27 K 3810—Brown. Shipping weight, 1 lb. 4 oz.

Sizes: 34 to 44 in. bust measure.

27 K 3824—Navy.
27 K 3825—Brown. Shipping weight, 1 lb. 2 oz.

27 K 3804—Colorful Stripes. Shpg. wt., 1 lb.

$1.29 Our Best Percale

80-square, washfast print! Fagotted white Cotton Pique trim.
Regular Sizes: 36 to 44, and Stout Sizes: 45 to 53 in. State size.

27 K 3788—Light Navy.
27 K 3789—Black and White. Shpg. wt., 1 lb.

Broadcloth button-back dress keeps you in style. *Fall & Winter 1935-1936*

Cotton Cordette dress frocks in plaids, stripes, florals, and prints. *Fall & Winter 1935-1936*

Never Before Such Values!
Superior Quality Cotton
CORDETTE
DRESS FROCKS
88¢ EACH
2 FOR $1⁶⁵

The Fabric You've Seen in $1²⁸ Dresses!
A Sears Sensation in Fashion and Fabric!
- Washfast
- Gorgeous Colors
- Exquisite Patterns

(A) **27 K 3860**—Fancy Plaid. White Cotton Pique trim. Sizes: 14 to 20 years to fit 32 to 38 in. bust measure. *State size.*

(B) **27 K 3874**—Colorful Fancy Stripes. Regular Sizes: 34 to 44, and Stout Sizes: 45 to 53 in. bust measure. *State size.*

(C) **27 K 3878**—Fancy Floral. Washfast Cotton Pique trim. Sizes: 32 to 40 in. bust measure. *State size.*

(D) **27 K 3864**—Navy and White Dot.
27 K 3865—Red and White Dot. Junior Sizes: 13 to 19 years. *State age-size.*

(E) **27 K 3870**—Med. Blue Print.
27 K 3871—Med. Green Print. White Cotton Pique trim. Sizes: 32 to 40 in. bust measure. *State size.*

(F) **27 K 4200**—Fancy Stripe. White Cotton Pique trim. Girls' Sizes: 8 to 14 years. *State age-size.*

(G) **27 K 4204**—Fancy Plaid. White Cotton Pique trim. Girls' Sizes: 8 to 14 years. *State age-size.*

Shpg. wt., each, 14 oz.

Button-Back
OOKS SMART
RONS FLAT

Reg. $1.98
Value!

Sears prove a
fast Broad
utility dres
keep up in
—and down i
Yoke top,
trim pockets!
action sleeve

Sizes: 32
in. bust. Sta

27 K 9501—
27 K 9502—
27 K 9503—

Shpg. wt.,

Lingerie

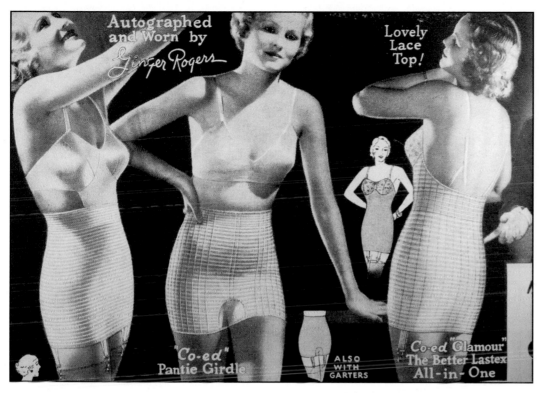

"Co-ed" corsetry with genuine 2-way Lastex stretch. *Spring & Summer 1935*

"Co-ed" girdles for young figures needing more control. *Spring & Summer 1935*

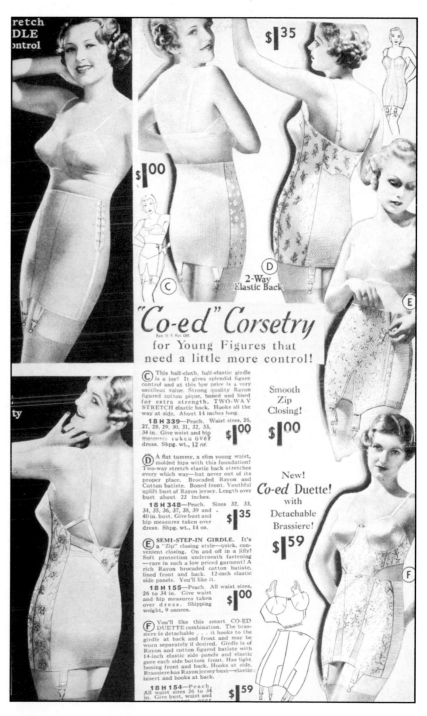

"Co-ed" Corsetry
for Young Figures that need a little more control!

C This half-cloth, half-elastic girdle is a joy! It gives splendid figure control and at this low price is a very excellent value. Strong quality Rayon figured cotton pique, boned and lined for extra strength. TWO-WAY STRETCH elastic back. Hooks all the way at side. About 14 inches long. **18 H 339**—Peach. Waist sizes, 26, 27, 28, 29, 30, 31, 32, 33, 34 in. Give waist and hip measures taken over dress. Shpg. wt., 12 oz. **$1.00**

D A flat tummy, a slim young waist, molded hips with this foundation! Two-way stretch elastic back stretches every which way—but never out of its proper place. Brocaded Rayon and Cotton batiste. Boned front. Youthful uplift bust of Rayon jersey. Length over bust about 22 inches. **18 H 348**—Peach. Sizes 32, 33, 34, 35, 36, 37, 38, 39 and 40 in. bust. Give bust and hip measures taken over dress. Shpg. wt., 14 oz. **$1.35**

E SEMI-STEP-IN GIRDLE. It's a "Zip" closing style—quick, convenient closing. On and off in a jiffy! Soft protection underneath fastening—rare in such a low priced garment! A rich Rayon brocaded cotton batiste, lined front and back. 12-inch elastic side panels. You'll like it. **18 H 155**—Peach. All waist sizes, 26 to 34 in. Give waist and hip measures taken over dress. Shipping weight, 9 ounces. **$1.00**

F You'll like this smart CO-ED DUETTE combination. The brassiere is detachable . . . it hooks to the girdle at back and front and may be worn separately if desired. Girdle is of Rayon and cotton figured batiste with 14-inch elastic side panels and elastic gore each side bottom front. Has light boning front and back. Hooks at side. Brassiere has Rayon jersey bust—elastic insert and hooks at back. **18 H 154**—Peach. All waist sizes 26 to 34 in. Give bust, waist size. **$1.59**

Smooth Zip Closing! **$1.00**

New! *Co-ed Duette!* with Detachable Brassiere! **$1.59**

2-Way Elastic Back

$1.35

$1.00

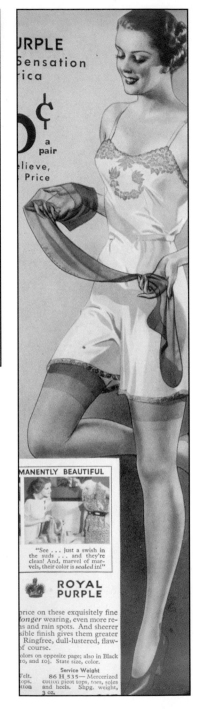

An autographed fashion worn in Hollywood by Loretta Young, this 4-in-1 garment takes the place of 4 separate pieces. Rayon knit chemises in two different styles. *Spring & Summer 1935*

Royal Purple silk stockings. *Spring & Summer 1935*

57c each
3 for $1.59

"DORABLES" OF CELANESE
Finely Tailored

Sears Famous
KNIT
RAYONS

$1.00 each

VEST OR BLOOMERS
89c each

Silk and Sanconize
TRICOT KNIT
Runproof

37c   39c   22c
New and Popular Briefs

Underwear in celanese and knit rayons. *Fall & Winter 1935-1936*

Silk Crepe

Rayon Taffeta

Rayon and Cotton Flat Crepe

A

B

Lace bottom silk crepe or rayon taffeta slips. *Fall & Winter 1935-1936*

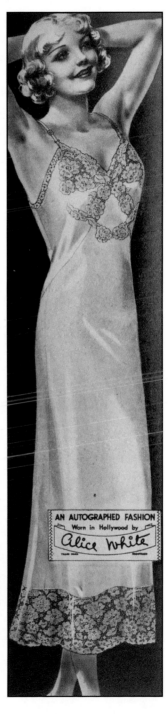

Worn in Hollywood by Alice White, pure dye satin slip has a wide lace bottom. *Fall & Winter 1935-1936*

AN AUTOGRAPHED FASHION
Worn in Hollywood by
Alice White

Rayon taffeta, silk crepe, and cotton broadcloth slips in California top, bodice top, and tailored styles.
Fall & Winter 1935-1936

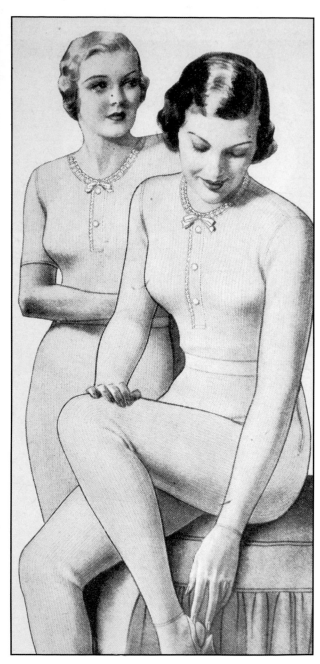

Rib stitched vests and drawers in medium weight cotton.
Fall & Winter 1935-1936

Pajamas

Pajamas in cotton broadcloth, terry cloth, sheer Batiste, and gay print styles.
Spring & Summer 1935

Cotton Broadcloth · Terry Cloth · Sheer Batiste · Gay Print

Also Stout Sizes

Our Smart "Co-ed" Robes

All wool flannel! "Co-ed" robe has hand drawn fringe belt. *Fall & Winter 1935-1936*

Shoes

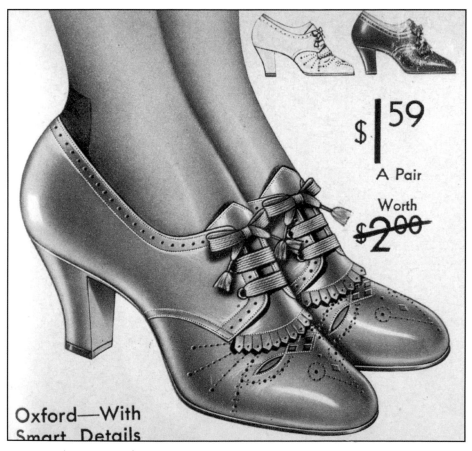

1^{59}

A Pair

Worth ~~$2^{00}~~

Oxford—With
Smart Details

Swanky oxfords with stylish 3-eye tie with a trim row of Kiltie fringing. Made of smooth elk grained leather. *Spring & Summer 1935*

LOW PRICES
FOR MAIL
ORDERS ONLY

1^{77}

A PAIR

Brand new oxford has dashing cut-outs, slashed tongue, rows of perforations, in fine-grained white or brown calf. *Spring & Summer 1935*

Autographed fashion worn in Hollywood by Joan Bennett. Smart shoe with tiny perforations in a dainty design. *Spring & Summer 1935*

Assorted sports shoes for girls provide comfort during sports activities. *Spring & Summer 1935*

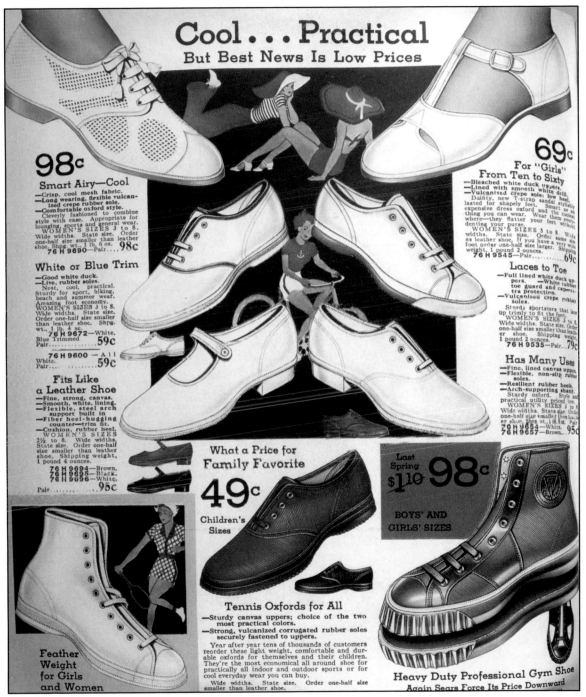

Sportswear

Regulation riding shirt and cotton whipcord jodhpurs, and genuine suede leather vest with cotton whipcord riding breeches. *Fall & Winter 1934*

3-piece sports outfit has skirt, shorts, and blouse in cotton fabric. Striped cotton 2-piece sports outfit has wrap-around skirt with combined shirt and shorts. *Spring & Summer 1935*

Jacket with matching hat in plaid gingham has Peter Pan collar and novelty buttons. Swanky sports jacket in cotton flannel is double breasted and belted back. *Spring & Summer 1935*

Whipcord breeches and jodhpurs are perfect for riding sports. *Spring & Summer 1935*

Misses' and Girls'
RIDING TOGS

Our Best All Wool Snowcloth
8⁹⁵

All Wool Special!
5⁹⁸

All wool suits are perfect for skating, skiing, hiking, or playing! *Fall & Winter 1935-1936*

Sweaters

All wool sweater in a fancy knit with deep patch pockets. Medium weight coat style sweater is rib stitched with a drop needle design. *Fall & Winter 1935-1936*

The Exciting Free Action Back $3.79

The very style worn by sport celebrities! It's the outstanding sweater fashion of the year. Our best choice in medium weight all wool zephyr, rib knit into a combination of style, high quality and usefulness. Belted effect; inverted pleats, back and front, that add to its sporty lines—so becoming for every use. Beautifully tailored.

Even Sizes, 34 to 44-in. bust. State size. Shipping weight, 1 lb. 7 oz.

38 K 7032—Navy Blue.

Shaker knit pullover sweater and cap in heavyweight all wool worsted fabric. Free action back sports sweater medium weight all wool zephyr. *Fall & Winter 1935-1936*

Fine Wools Make Them Better!

(A) Big Bargain! All Wool!
Actually priced 20% lower this year! Practical All Wool, firmly knit, cardigan stitch. Medium heavy weight. Even Sizes, 34 to 44 in. bust. State size. Shipping weight, 2 lbs.

38 K 7027 Dark Red
38 K 7025 Buff
38 K 7026 Navy Blue
$1.98

(B) Convertible Neck!
Warm All Wool Worsted sweater coat with rib drop stitch. Medium weight. The handiest all-purpose garment. Now at a new low price. Even Sizes, 34 to 44-in. bust. State size. Shipping weight, 1 lb. 4 oz.

38 K 7274 Monkey Skin
38 K 7273 Black
38 K 7276 Medium Blue
$2.39

(C) All Wool Zephyr
Soft and Warm. Extra fine quality with slightly brushed surface. Medium weight. Expert tailoring. Even Sizes, 34 to 44-in. bust. State size. Shipping weight, 1 lb. 4 oz.

38 K 7152 Tile Red
38 K 7155 Natural (Camel Tan)
38 K 7156 Black
$2.98

(D) All Wool Worsted
Rarely found at this price! Firm smart rib stitch. Medium weight. Seams and shoulders carefully finished. Ideal also for under-the-coat wear. Even Sizes, 34 to 44-in. bust. State size. Shpg. wt., 1 lb. 3 oz.

38 K 7037 Medium Brown
38 K 7038 Navy Blue
38 K 7039 Medium Blue
$1.98

All wool sweaters in trendy styles. *Fall & Winter 1935-1936*

Sweaters in a wide selection of color and styles. All wool two-piece ski suit. Zip front knitted brushed sport jacket. *Fall & Winter 1935-1936*

Plaids are Smart! ¼ Wool Worsted CHOICE **$1.00** each   Gay Stripes All Wool Worsted

Brushed Slip-On "Zip" Closing

"Zip" Fastener Opens all the way

Knitted Brushed SPORT JACKET **$1.98**

Knit ALL WOOL 2-Piece Ski-Suit **$5.95**

Ski Pants only **$2.69**

All Wool Worsted (F) **$1.48**

Our Best Girls' Pullover! **$1.69**

A Special Bargain! **75c**

GIRLS TWIN SWEATER SE

All Wool Worsted **$1.98**

Here's Style — and lots of it — For Schoolgirls!

Ribbed Stitch (N) All Wool Worsted **$1.95**

All Wool **$1.89**   Part Wool **$1.49**   Fine Cotton **$1.19**   All Wool Shaker Coat **$2.39**   Brushed Wool Sweater **$1.00**   Tam **29c**   All Wool **49c** each

138   For descriptions and other colors see opposite page

Girls Fashions

Coats

Matching novelty weave coat and beret, all wool Cheviot coat and beret, and checked coat and beret has a velveteen collar. *Spring & Summer 1936*

Girls coat with matching hat and muff has real Beaver-dyed lamb fur. Chinchilla cloth coat with matching beret. All wool Polo coats. Chinchilla coat with or without fur has matching beret. Velour coat with or without fur has matching beret. *Fall & Winter 1934*

Coat with detachable cape in a beautiful tweed mixture of wool and silk Noil. Mother and daughter can both have this same coat. *Spring & Summer 1935*

Wide selection of girls' coats with matching berets. *Spring & Summer 1935*

All wool Polo coat for mom and daughter, or big and little sisters! *Spring & Summer 1935*

91

All Wool Coat and Hat

$6⁴⁸

Muff $1²⁹

With Laskin Lamb Fur

The "Little Princess" coat! Smart belted and box-pleated back. Warm *All Wool* Fleece. Soft beaver-like Laskin Lamb Fur collar. Sateen yoke. Cotton plaid lining. Hat to match.
Ages: 6, 7, 8, 9 and 10 years. *State age-size.*
17 K 4625—Lt. Brown.
17 K 4626—Med. Blue. $6.48
17 K 4627—Winetone.
Shipping weight, 3 lbs. 4 oz.

Laskin Lamb Fur Muff
Rayon and cotton lined.
17 K 4797—Beaver $1.29
Brown.

Coat, Hat and Muff Set

$4⁹⁸ UP

Thick curly nap makes this Persian Lamb Fur Fabric exceptionally warm! Wool and Rayon pile on a strong cotton back. Lined with thick cotton suede cloth. Sateen lined sleeves. Imitation leather belt. Hat, coat and muff set. *State age.*
Ages: 6, 7, 8, 9 years.
17 K 4630— Light Brown. $4.98
17 K 4631— Medium Gray. Set

Ages: 10, 12 and 14 years.
17 K 4530— Light Brown. $5.98
17 K 4531— Medium Gray. Set
Shipping weight, each, 3 lbs. 8 oz.

Ages 6 to 9

Ages 10 to 14

"Little Princess" coat and hat set is all wool fleece with beaver-like Laskin lamb fur collar. Persian lamb fur fabric coat, hat, and muff set. *Fall & Winter 1935-1936*

SIZE SCALE FOR GIRLS' COATS
Ages: 6 · 7 · 8 · 9 · 10-12-14-16 years.
Chest: 25-26-27-28-29-31-33-35 inches.
Length: 27-28-30-32-34-37-39-43 inches.

STURDY WINTER COATING
Ages 6 to 9 $3⁴⁸
Ages 10 to 14 $4⁴⁸

(A) The thick, fur-like pile certainly does keep breezes out! And body warmth *in!* "Cozy Pelt," a velvety-soft cotton fabric, lined with thick cotton suede cloth. Sleeves sateen lined.
Coat with Beret to Match
Ages: 6, 7, 8, 9 years.
State age-size.
17 K 4610—Polo Tan.
17 K 4612—Med. Gray. $2.98
Ages: 10, 12, 14 years.
State age-size.
17 K 4510—Polo Tan.
17 K 4511—Logwood Brown.
17 K 4512—Med. Gray. $3.65
Shipping weight, each, 3 lbs. 12 oz.

(B) A grand value! Thick coating, more than half Wool, balance Rayon and Cotton. The wool is in the nap where it shows, the cotton in the lengthwise threads for strength! Warmly lined with Cotton Suede Cloth; sleeves lined with sateen. *State age-size.*
Ages: 6, 7, 8, 9 years.
17 K 4615—Navy Blue.
17 K 4616—Dark Brown.
17 K 4617—Winetone. $3.48
Ages: 10, 12 and 14 years.
17 K 4515—Navy Blue.
17 K 4516—Dark Brown. $4.48
Shipping weight, each, 3 lbs. 10 oz.

"Cozy Pelt" Coat and Beret to Match
Ages 6 to 9 $2⁹⁸ SET
Ages 10 to 14 $3⁶⁵ SET

All garments on this page are sent direct from New York to you, but you pay postage only from our nearest Mail Order House.

WARM COATING with Fur Fabric Collar and Muff
Ages 10 to 16 $5⁹⁸ SET

Big wide revers and muff with the richness of effect and warmth of fur! They're Cozy-Pelt, a thick cotton pile fabric! Coat is a warm three-fifths Wool fabric. Lining of gay cotton Plaid has sateen yoke.
Ages: 10 to 16 years.
State age-size.
17 K 4525—Med. Brown with Tan Fur Fabric.
17 K 4526—Navy with Gray Fur Fabric.
17 K 4527—Winetone with Tan Fur Fabric.
Shipping wt., 5 lbs.

All Wool MELTON
Ages 6 to 9 $4⁷⁴
Ages 10 to 14 $5⁷⁴

Attractively stitched, smartly styled, double-breasted coat of finer quality warm All Wool Melton. Warmly lined with Cotton Suede Cloth.
Ages: 6, 7, 8, 9 years. *State age-size.*
17 K 4620—Navy Blue.
17 K 4621—Dark Brown. $4.74
Shipping weight, 3 lbs. 8 oz.
Ages: 10, 12 and 14 years. *State age-size.*
17 K 4520—Navy Blue.
17 K 4521—Dark Brown. $5.74
Shipping weight, 4 lbs. 2 oz.

"Cozy Pelt" coat is velvety soft lined with thick cotton cloth. "Cozy Pelt" coat and beret set. "Cozy Pelt" with fur fabric collar and muff. All wool Melton coat lined with cotton suede cloth. *Fall & Winter 1935-1936*

Charming Shirley Temple fashions for girls. All wool fleece snow suit with hat in one-piece style. Three-piece all wool fleece Herringbone coat, legging, and hat set. *Fall & Winter 1935-1936*

Shirley Temple fashions come in an all wool three-piece suit, all wool coat and hat set, and a Bolero ensemble. *Fall & Winter 1935-1936*

These
The m
is exqu
and th
dresses
her lat

38 K 5
38 K 5
Ship

S

This fa
body f
ribbon
78 K 6
78 K 6
21¼ in

Two- and three-piece suits in fabrics such as cotton suede cloth, all wool flannel, cotton fleece, and chinchilla cloth. *Fall & Winter 1935-1936*

Dresses

Lovely girls dress for ages 8 to 14. *Spring & Summer 1936*

Pajamas

Colorful outfits for children in an array of styles. *Spring & Summer 1935*

One- and two-piece cotton pajamas in prints and solids. *Spring & Summer 1935*

Play Clothes

Regulation Middy **75¢**

Two-Piece Playsuit **95¢**

Pleated Skirt **98¢**

For Sports—Middy Slacks and Hat **$1.59** Complete

The Cossack For Sports **$1.25**

Cotton Broadcloth

Two-piece playsuit has blue sailor collar with braid trim. Regulation middy in cotton jean cloth with white cotton broadcloth bodice. Sailor outfit in cotton Linene with contrasting tie. Cossack jacket in cotton flannel. *Spring & Summer 1935*

"Sunshine" play clothes are so healthful for little ones. *Spring & Summer 1935*

All wool overall leggings, cotton fleece plaid top suit, beacon cotton chinchilla suit, and all wool suits keep them warm at playtime. *Fall & Winter 1935-1936*

(A) Wear Under Coat or Over Sweater **$1.98** All Wool "OVERALL" LEGGINGS

FOR DESCRIPTIONS SEE OPPOSITE PAGE

1 to 3 Years

Tots like them Smart, too!

(B) Cotton Fleece Plaid Top **$1.98** SET

(C) Beacon Cotton Chinchilla **$2.89** SET

(D) **$4.98** SET

(E) **$5.65** SET

Shoes

Fringe Trim

—**Serviceable leather uppers.**
—**Smooth leather quarter lining.**
—**Serviceable rugged leather sole.**
Swagger style for school girls and boys. Smart perforated design.
Girls' and Boys' Sizes 8½ to 3. Wide widths. State size. Shipping weight, 1 pound 4 ounces.
15 K 1055—Black.
15 K 1071—Brown Mandrucca Leather, Brown Calf
Trim..............Pair, **$1.49**

Autographed fashion worn in Hollywood by Cora Sue Collins, these shoes are a swagger style for school. *Fall & Winter 1935-1936*

89c A Pair
Shoes Give Ankle Support
—Good grade, long wearing soft leather uppers for baby's feet.
—Flexible, stitchdown leather soles help him walk more easily.
Proper shoes for their first steps make such a big difference. Start your youngster properly in these. Roomy, foot form last.
Babies' Sizes 2 to 6. Wide widths. State size. Shpg. wt., 8 oz.
15 H 312—Smoke Color.
15 H 313—Patent Leather. **89c**
15 H 314—White Leather.
15 H 437—Black Leather.

—Patent Leather. —Stitchdown leather soles.
Babies' Sizes 2 to 6. Wide widths. State size. Shipping weight, 8 ounces.
15 H 521—Pair......**69c**

—Patent leather. —Stitchdown leather soles.
Babies' Sizes 2 to 6. Wide widths. State size. Shipping weight, 7 ounces.
15 H 511—Reduced to **79c**

—Good grade leather soles. Fine support for first steps.
Babies' Sizes 2 to 6. Wide widths. State size. Shipping weight, 8 ounces.
15 H 488—Pair......**95c**

Two Tone Smoke Color Leather

FIRST STEPS SIZES 2 TO 6
TEETER REG. U.S. PAT. OFF.

ALL PRICES FOR MAIL ORDERS ONLY

59c

Leather Sole
—White leather with pebble grained leather strap or black patent leather with beige color leather strap.
Babies' Sizes 2 to 6. Wide widths. State size. Shipping weight, 8 ounces.
15 H 517—White
15 H 518—Patent. Pair, **89c**

—Sturdy leather uppers.
—Stitchdown leather soles.
—Correct foot form last. Neat well made bluchers.
Babies' Sizes 2 to 6. Wide widths. State size. Shipping weight, 6 ounces. Reduced Price.
15 H 486—Patent.
15 H 496—Smoke......**69c**

—Trim 2-strap sandal with cut-outs and perforations.
—Long wearing leather sole.
—Stitchdown construction.
Babies' Sizes 2 to 6. Wide widths. State size. Shipping weight, 9 ounces.
15 H 515—White
15 H 516—Smoke. Pair, **89c**

—Patent leather with gray reptile design applique.
—Serviceable leather soles.
—Stitchdown construction.
Babies' Sizes 2 to 6. Wide widths. State size. Shipping weight, 8 ounces.
15 H 520—Pair......**69c**

—Black kid, soft and pliable.
—Pretty stitching on vamp.
—Hand turned leather sole, extremely flexible.
Babies' Sizes 2 to 5. Wide widths. State size. Shipping weight, 8 ounces.
15 H 519—Pair......**59c**

69c

49c
SEE PAGE 264 FOR HOW TO MEASURE

79c

A wide selection of Teeter Totter shoes for girls in many styles. *Spring & Summer 1935*

Undergarments

Wool and cotton vest with rayon stripes. Vest, bloomers, and panties in medium weight cotton. Rayon striped cotton vest and panties. *Fall & Winter 1935-1936*

Flatter-ees vests, panties, and union suits for girls. *Fall & Winter 1935-1936*

Men's Fashions

Casual

Extra heavy sweater in wool worsted woolen yarn with a double shawl collar. Wool worsted sweater in medium weight. Sporty fancy stitch medium weight sweater in all wool. *Fall & Winter 1934*

Army style warm flannel shirt has a lined chest and double elbows for warmth. Double napped suede cloth shirt is heavy weight with a quick action fastener front. Medium heavy weight sacking flannel is big and roomy with unbreakable buttons. Buffalo checked shirt is all wool flannel with extra strong tailoring. *Fall & Winter 1934*

All wool Cassimere slacks with a one-button waistband with doggy new deep tunnel belt loops and striking tabs that button over top and hip pockets. *Fall & Winter 1934*

Sanforized cotton nub slacks are cool, dressy, and comfortable. *Spring & Summer 1935*

Pepperell blue and white pinch check or pinstripe slacks. Shrinkproof sturdy cotton covert slacks. *Spring & Summer 1935*

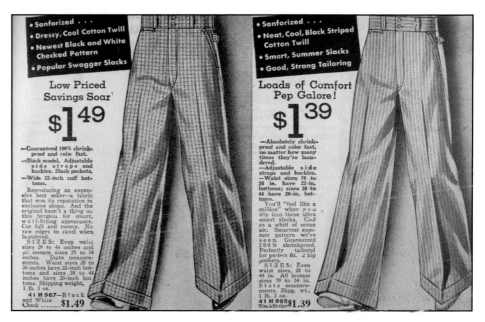

- Sanforized . . .
- Dressy, Cool Cotton Twill
- Newest Black and White Checked Pattern
- Popular Swagger Slacks

Low Priced Savings Soar'

$1⁴⁹

—Guaranteed 100% shrink-proof and color fast.
—Slack model. Adjustable side straps and buckles. Slash pockets.
—Wide 22-inch cuff bottoms.

Reproducing an expensive best seller—a fabric that won its reputation in exclusive shops. And the original hasn't a thing on this bargain for smart, well-fitting appearance. Cut full and roomy. No raw edges to ravel when laundered.
SIZES: Even waist sizes 28 to 44 inches and all inseam sizes 29 to 34 inches. State measurements. Waist sizes 28 to 36 inches have 22-inch bottoms and sizes 38 to 44 inches have 20-inch bottoms. Shipping weight, 1 lb. 3 oz.
41 H 967—Black and White Check $1.49

- Sanforized . . .
- Neat, Cool, Black Striped Cotton Twill
- Smart, Summer Slacks
- Good, Strong Tailoring

Loads of Comfort Pep Galore!

$1³⁹

—Absolutely shrink-proof and color fast, no matter how many times they're laundered.
—Adjustable side straps and buckles.
—Waist sizes 28 to 35 in. have 22-in. bottoms; sizes 38 to 44 have 20-in. bottoms.

You'll "feel like a million" when you slip into these ultra smart slacks. Cool as a whiff of ocean air. Smartest summer pattern we've seen. Guaranteed 100% shrinkproof. Perfectly tailored for perfect fit. 2 hip pockets.
SIZES: Even waist sizes, 28 to 44 in. All inseam sizes 29 to 34 in. State measurements. Shpg. wt., 1 lb. 3 oz.
41 H 965—BlackStripe .$1.39

Sanforized cotton twill slacks in black and white checked pattern. Black striped cotton twill slacks have good tailoring. *Spring & Summer 1935*

World Beater for Price
Sturdy Cotton Covert

98c

—Guaranteed 100% shrinkproof.
—Extra strong, cool and comfortable. Easy to launder.
—Strongly constructed.
—20-inch cuff bottoms.

Regardless how low the price, here's the quality you can trust. Wash 'em. Soak 'em. Rub 'em. THEY WON'T SHRINK. Cool, sturdy Covert Cloth. Good looking and decidedly popular pattern. Styled for neat appearance. Cut full and roomy. No raw edges to unravel when laundered. Not skimped in any way to make this price. For our Best covert pants see page 347.

SIZES: Even waist sizes, 28 to 44 inches; all inseam sizes, 29 to 34 inches. State measurements. Shipping weight, 1 lb. 1 oz.

41 H 834—Oxford Gray 98c

On all Shrinkproof Pants, order your exact size.

Moleskin cloth pants in neat black or gray striped pattern. *Spring & Summer 1935*

Long sleeve and sleeveless sweaters, twin sweater sets, and vests for men. *Fall & Winter 1935-1936*

Cotton suede cloth shirt is napped on both sides. Double napped cotton suede cloth shirt with Talon slide fastener. Moleskin cloth shirt in heavyweight cotton and Talon slide fastener. *Fall & Winter 1935-1936*

Flannel shirt has a double chest for warmth and double elbows for wear. *Fall & Winter 1935-1936*

Warm wool sweaters in smart, popular styles. *Fall & Winter 1935-1936*

Coats

Moleskin cloth coat is sheepskin lined with a half wool knit collar and cuffs, button front, and pockets reinforced and faced with genuine leather. *Fall & Winter 1934*

Horsehide coat with thick woolly sheepskin lining and wombat sheepskin collar has non-breakable Bakelite buttons. *Fall & Winter 1934*

"Indestructo" jackets in leather-like cotton suede or medium heavy navy blue mackinaw cloth. *Spring & Summer 1935*

4^{98}

Guaranteed
100% WATERPROOF

CHICAGO REGULATION
POLICE STYLE
VENTILATED
ALL AROUND
DOUBLE CAPE

Full 52
Inches Long

Hercules storm kings are vulcanized to a strong cotton base, all seams are wide lapped, stitched, cemented and steam vulcanized. Side slash pockets in roomy patterns. *Spring & Summer 1935*

Sporty two-color jacket with all wool fancy back. Genuine suede leather Cossack jacket. *Fall & Winter 1935-1936*

Buck Skein polo coat in leatherlike cotton suede. Small check cotton coat with vulcanized rubber on a fast color plaid lining. Stylemaker suede-like cotton is smooth as velvet and wears like leather. *Spring & Summer 1935*

DOUBLE PURPOSE
RAIN OR SHINE

5^{85}
Colorful

7^{45}

Mackinaw all wool cloth coat in striking 3-color plaid pattern. Hudson Bay type all wool mackinaw in dark brown with light tan stripe. *Fall & Winter 1935-1936*

Cotton suede coat has fleece lining with several layers of pure gum rubber. Leather-like cotton suede with orange cotton flannel lining. Cotton suede Cossack jacket is lined with cotton flannel in novel leopard skin design. *Fall & Winter 1935-1936*

Hound's Tooth checks are found on suede-like triple texture cotton fabric coat with handsome plaid cotton lining. Buckskein coat in leather-like cotton suede is treated with a Du-Pont process that makes it waterproof. Guardsmean coat is made of light tan cotton twill Gabardine with a cotton plaid lining. *Fall & Winter 1935-1936*

Moleskin cloth coat with deep pile sheepskin lining and a large shawl collar of American Wombat. Wale corduroy has sheepskin lining and a big wide shawl collar of American Wombat. *Fall & Winter 1935-1936*

Brown or blue all wool coats in the latest fall style. *Fall & Winter 1935-1936*

All wool Melton coat in the new 3-button double breasted style. All wool coat in check pattern. All wool coat with contrasting shade pearl-like buttons. *Fall & Winter 1935-1936*

Hats

Smart assortment of hats in the latest styles. *Spring & Summer 1935*

Hats can be worn to advantage by men of all ages. *Spring & Summer 1936*

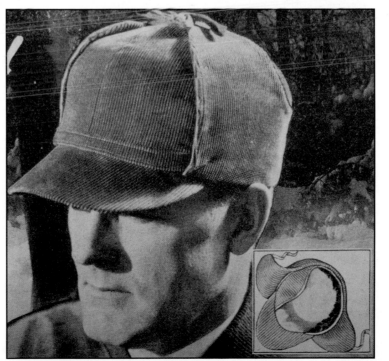

Sportsman's ribbed corduroy hat has a top that can be turned down and tied under the chin, turned down fur lined ear flaps, and a sturdy canvas visor. *Fall & Winter 1935-1936*

Shoes

Men's Gold Bond shoes in a variety of handsome styles including the Moccasin Toe Sportster, Novelty High Stepper, Southern Tie, The Jumbo, The Aristocrat, The Promenader, The Streeter, and The Wales. *Fall & Winter 1934*

Good Luck shoes resist moisture and barnyard acids with stay soft uppers that remain pliable through grueling days of work. *Spring & Summer 1934*

Good Lucks leather uppers have oak-tanned oil treated band leather outsoles for long wear, and have brass nail reinforcement on the toe and shank. *Spring & Summer 1936*

Good Luck boots are made of genuine Cordovan horsehide. Green Grip boots have genuine Goodyear construction. Leather upper boots in brown leather, natural, and elk-grained black. *Fall & Winter 1934*

WAS $1⁸⁹   WAS $1⁸⁹

"Trouser Crease" in Goodyear welt with chrome-tanned leather upper. French Toe in fine, chrome-tanned black side leather upper with Goodyear welt. Broad toe shoe has genuine Goodyear welt with black side leather uppers. *Spring & Summer 1935*

Good looking black kid-skin uppers with genuine Goodyear welts. These shoes are soft and comfortable. *Spring & Summer 1935*

.59

Steel
Arch Support

$2⁷⁹ $2⁷⁹

Leather shoes in solids and two-tone colors. *Spring & Summer 1935*

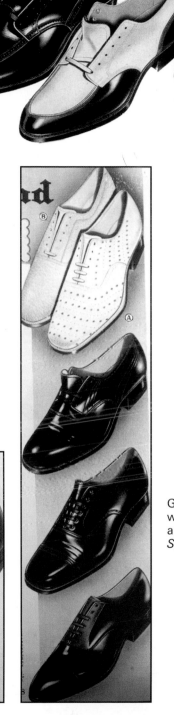

Gold Bond shoes have Goodyear welts, fine-quality leather uppers and insoles, and oak leather soles. *Spring & Summer 1935*

Kangaroo shoes in Blucher and Bal styles with genuine Goodyear welts and Goodyear wing-foot rubber heels. Shod Rite in white or black leather with Goodyear welts. *Spring & Summer 1935*

Good Luck shoes and boots are tough with oak tanned, oil-treated, bend leather soles, in brown or black. *Spring & Summer 1935*

Service leather shoes are tough and dressy. *Spring & Summer 1935*

Famous Stitchdowns in steel arch, compo, and double sewed sole styles. All leather English style boots have fine leather uppers, oak-tanned leather sole, and Goodyear welt. *Spring & Summer 1935*

Barnyard acid resisting work shoes have re-tanned leather uppers, Goodyear wing-foot outsoles, grain leather insoles, live 13-nail rubber heels, and comfort! *Spring & Summer 1935*

Work boots in a variety of lengths and styles are tough to help you get your job done. *Spring & Summer 1935*

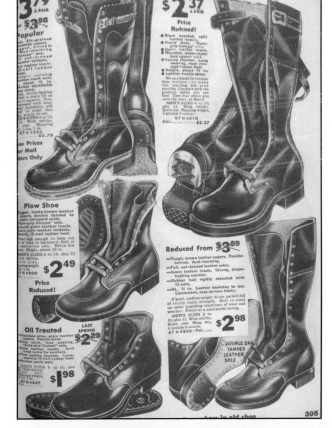

Flint-Rock boots are built up layer by layer for maximum tough-ness. *Spring & Summer 1935*

Moccasin style shoes with Goodyear welt. Wing Tip Walker shoes with Goodyear welt. *Fall & Winter 1935-1936*

Johnson's Kangaroo shoes offer super comfort. *Fall & Winter 1935-1936*

The Kangaroo, a marvelous animal. A more marvelous leather. TOUGH and SINEWY.

$3.89 Pair

Johnson's Kangaroo

TWO FULL OAK TANNED LEATHER SOLES

Last Fall $3.59

Big, Burly Strength

Barnyard acid resisting black or brown boots. *Fall & Winter 1935-1936*

KANGAROO

★ LIGHT
★ STRONG
★ FLEXIBLE
★ COMFORTABLE

$3.98 A PAIR

The Australian Kangaroo...famous for his TOUGH hide.

Choice of Two Styles
● Oak tanned bend leather outsole.
● Buffed grain leather insole.
● Narrow arch-hugging heel.
● Goodyear Wingfoot rubber heel.
● Genuine Goodyear Welt.

It's not ordinary Kangaroo, but four-star—the strongest of all known leathers! As restful as an old slipper and as fine wearing a shoe as you could ask. Because the fibres are interlaced it's hard to scuff. Takes an unusually brilliant polish. Perhaps you've seen similar models in high priced shops. Sears might logically ask a dollar more for these!

Today's Value $5.00

The Shoe
67 K 4222—Wide (E) Bal
67 K 4223—Narrow (C) Bal
67 K 4220—Wide (E) Blucher
67 K 4221—Narrow (C) Blucher

The Oxford
67 K 4486—Wide (E) Bal
67 K 4487—Narrow (C) Bal
67 K 4480—Wide (E) Blucher
67 K 4481—Narrow (C) Blucher
MEN'S SIZES: 5 to 11; also 12. State size. Shipping weight, shoes, 2 pounds 8 ounces; oxfords, 2 pounds 6 ounces.

Bal Style

Blucher Style

It's Ea to be Fitt See Page

Kangaroo shoes in Bal-style or Blucher style. *Fall & Winter 1935-1936*

SPECIAL VALUE
Mud King
① Duck Chafer Stay
② Tire Cord Back Stay
③ Kickoff Heel

Exceptional low price for quality so high! Heavy bumper edge sole. Fleece lining. All-around foxing—reinforcing at all strain points—waterproof clear to top! Barnyard proof—acid resisting! Built of alternate layers of hard wearing black rubber and long wearing fabric. Black sole.
Wide widths. State size. Order same size as ordinary weight shoes or one size larger than heavy work shoes.
MEN'S AND BIG BOYS' SIZES 6 to 12. No half sizes. Shipping weight, 3 pounds 4 ounces.
76 K 9286—Pair....$2.29

Today's Value $2.75 $2.29

Mud Washes Right Off

—Alternate plies of sturdy fabric and black rubber.
—Full gusset, waterproof to top.
—Extra heavy bumper edge sole.
—Chafing strip.
Wide widths. State size. Order same size as ordinary weight shoes or one size larger than heavy work shoes.
MEN'S SIZES 6 to 13. No half sizes. Shipping wt., 5 lbs. 4 oz. $2.09
76 K 9258—Pair....
BOYS'

—Heavy black Gibraltar arctic.
—Outer ply of strong TUF-TWILL
—Fleece lined.—Full gusset, closed clear to the top.
—Heavy, long-service outsole.
Wide widths. State size. Order same size as ordinary weight shoes or one size larger than heavy work shoes.
MEN'S SIZES 6 to 13. No half sizes. Shipping wt., 4 lbs. 5 oz. $2.09
76 K 9256—Pair....
BOYS' SIZES 1 to 6. No half sizes.

Gibraltar mud resisting boots in sturdy fabric or black rubber. Mud King boots have fleece lining and are built of layers of hard wearing black rubber and long wearing fabric. *Fall & Winter 1935-1936*

Suits

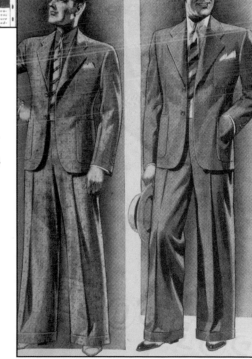

White cotton suit with smart black nubs is Sanforized so it won't shrink. Light weight all wool tropical worsted suit is comfortable and cool. *Spring & Summer 1935*

All wool dark blue surge suit lined in Earl Glo rayon, dark blue cheviot in a faint Herringbone pattern, fine twill all-wool blue serge suit, and a fashion tailored Skinner Satin lined serge suit. *Spring & Summer 1934*

113

Pure virgin wool worsted suit is luxuriously lined with Earl-Glo rayon. 2-button notch lapel with handmade button holes and buttons sewed on by hand with waxed linen thread. A fine suit. *Spring & Summer 1935*

One button peaked lapel model suit has high cushion shoulders, luxurious blue cheviot, subdued Herringbone weave, fancy checked wool flannel double breasted reversible vest, and wide 22-inch trousers. *Spring & Summer 1935*

A variety of men's suits in the new styles of 1935. *Spring & Summer 1935*

STRATHMORE CLOTHES

The Ultimate in Value at...

$14.75

Strathmore suits in fine all wool hand finished worsted fabric, all wool silk striped worsted, and all virgin wool diamond weave worsted fabrics. *Spring & Summer 1935*

Virgin wool silk striped worsted suit with coat lined in Earl-Glo rayon. All wool cassimere suit has the new 2-button peaked lapel. *Spring & Summer 1935*

Strathmore brand suit in a choice of pure virgin wool blue serge or dark oxford gray all wool worsted. Swagger style suit in all wool and worsted cheviot in subdued herringbone weave. Blue serge suit in all wool fabric. Virgin wool blue serge suit has superb tailoring. *Fall & Winter 1935-1936*

An assortment of suits for men offer the latest styles. *Fall & Winter 1935-1936*

All wool cassimere brown suit. All virgin wool diamond weave worsted suit. Pure virgin wool worsted suit with an attractive silk striped pattern. *Fall & Winter 1935-1936*

Undergarments

MESH SUITS

57c each

Short Sleeves . . . Ankle length

So Cool . . . So Low Priced

They're Always Summer Favorites

Athletic Styles

52c each

Mesh suits in extra fine cotton that let the body breathe. *Spring & Summer 1935*

BETTER QUALITY

Combed Cotton

Better In FABRIC In FIT . . . In MAKING

Pilgrim **BRAND SPRING NEEDLE KNIT**

95c each suit

BUTTON on SHOULDER Suits . .

KEEP COOL in an **"AIR COOL"**

It Laughs at Summer Heat

NOW **69c** each

Pilgrim Brand
Reg. U.S. Pat. Off.

Was 79c

Fine, Strong 2-Ply Lisle

Combed Cotton

"Pilgrim" 2-ply Lisle and Swiss ribbed suits keep you cool in the summer months. *Spring & Summer 1935*

"Pilgrim" spring needle knit suit in combed cotton. *Spring & Summer 1935*

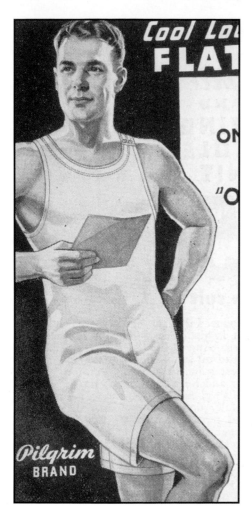

Flat knit suit with button shoulder in cool lightweight cotton. *Spring & Summer 1935*

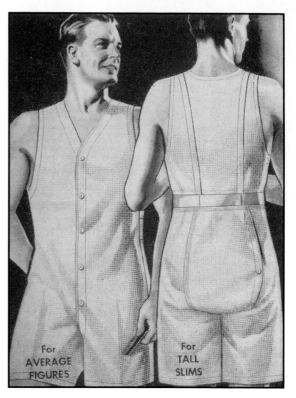

"Pilgrim" nainsook summer suits with elastic snubber in back and neat bar-tacking. *Spring & Summer 1935*

Button front or button shoulder cool rayon suits. *Spring & Summer 1935*

Pajamas and Robes

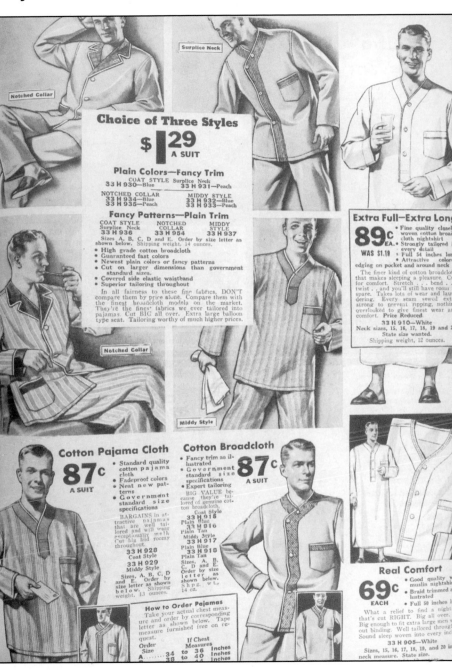

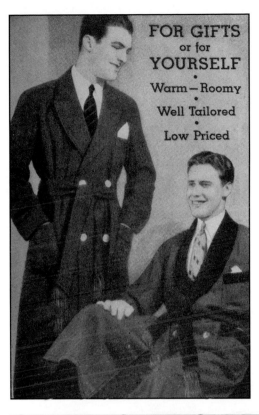

Choice of Three Styles

$1 29 A SUIT

Plain Colors—Fancy Trim

COAT STYLE Surplice Neck
33 H 930—Blue   33 H 931—Peach

NOTCHED COLLAR   MIDDY STYLE
33 H 934—Blue   33 H 932—Blue
33 H 935—Peach   33 H 933—Peach

Fancy Patterns—Plain Trim

COAT STYLE   NOTCHED   MIDDY
Surplice Neck   COLLAR   STYLE
33 H 936   33 H 954   33 H 937

Sizes, A, B, C, D and E. Order by size letter as shown below. Shipping weight, 14 ounces.

- High grade cotton broadcloth
- Guaranteed fast colors
- Newest plain colors or fancy patterns
- Cut on larger dimensions than government standard sizes.
- Covered side elastic waistband
- Superior tailoring throughout

In all fairness to these fine fabrics, DON'T compare them by price alone. Compare them with the finest broadcloth models on the market. They're the finest fabrics we ever tailored into pajamas. Cut BIG all over. Extra large balloon type seat. Tailoring worthy of much higher prices.

Notched Collar

Surplice Neck

Middy Style

Extra Full—Extra Long

89¢ EA.

WAS $1.19

- Fine quality closely woven cotton broadcloth nightshirt
- Strongly tailored in every detail
- Full 54 inches long
- Attractive colored edging on pocket and around neck

The finer kind of cotton broadcloth that makes sleeping a pleasure. Cut for comfort. Stretch . . . bend . . . twist . . and you'll still have room to spare. Takes lots of wear and laundering. Every seam sewed extra strong to prevent ripping, nothing overlooked to give finest wear and comfort. Price Reduced.

33 H 910—White
Neck sizes, 15, 16, 17, 18, 19 and 20.
State size wanted.
Shipping weight, 12 ounces.

Cotton Pajama Cloth

87¢ A SUIT

- Standard quality cotton pajama cloth
- Fadeproof colors
- Neat new patterns
- Government standard size specifications

BARGAINS in attractive pajamas that are well tailored and will wear exceptionally well. Cut big and roomy throughout.

33 H 928
Coat Style
33 H 929
Middy Style

Sizes, A, B, C, D and E. Order by size letter as shown below. Shipping weight, 13 ounces.

Cotton Broadcloth

87¢ A SUIT

- Fancy trim as illustrated
- Government standard size specifications
- Expert tailoring

BIG VALUE because they're tailored of genuine cotton broadcloth.

Coat Style
33 H 915
Plain Blue
33 H 916
Plain Tan
Middy Style
33 H 917
Plain Blue
33 H 918
Plain Tan

Sizes, A, B, C, D and E. Order by size letter as shown below. Shpg. wt., 14 oz.

Real Comfort

69¢ EACH

- Good quality white muslin nightshirt
- Braid trimmed as illustrated
- Full 50 inches long

What a relief to find a nightshirt that's cut RIGHT. Big all over. Big enough to fit extra large men without binding. Well tailored throughout. Sound sleep woven into every inch.

33 H 905—White
Sizes, 15, 16, 17, 18, 19, and 20 inch neck measure. State size.

How to Order Pajamas

Take your actual chest measure and order by corresponding letter as shown below. Tape measure furnished free on request.

Order Size		If Chest Measures		
A	34	to	36	Inches
	38	to	40	Inches
			44	Inches

Wide selection of men's pajamas and nightshirts. *Spring & Summer 1935*

FOR GIFTS or for YOURSELF

- Warm – Roomy
- Well Tailored
- Low Priced

All wool flannel double-breasted robe has a wide fringe tasseled sash. "St. Moritz" all wool flannel robe with contrasting trim and knotted fringe sash. *Fall & Winter 1935-1936*

Cotton flannel pajamas in medium and heavy weights. *Fall & Winter 1935-1936*

Shirts

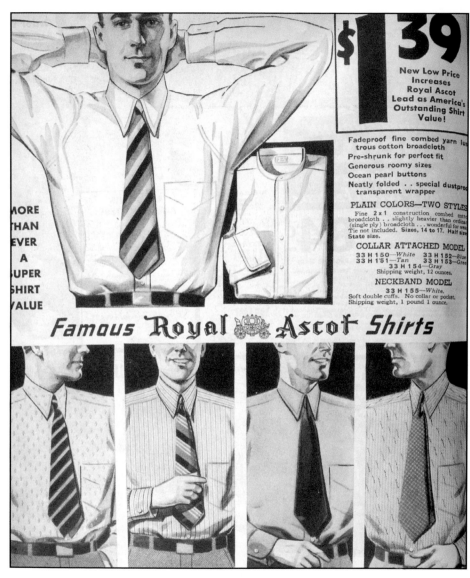

Famous Royal Ascot shirts in solids, prints, and all-over patterns. *Spring & Summer 1935*

Pre-shrunk cotton broadcloth shirts in plain or patterns. *Fall & Winter 1935-1936*

Swimwear

Fit-Rite Speed suit, high waisted trunk and speed shirt, and zip top suit for men and boys. *Spring & Summer 1935*

Work Clothes

Hercules overalls have 16 work tested features and come with a lifetime guarantee. *Spring & Summer 1934*

Absorbent, durable, and comfortable. Work shirt In medium-weight chambray lined with cotton sheeting, triple stitched at all important seams, with unbreakable buttons. *Spring & Summer 1935*

Covert outfit with all matching pants, shirt, and hat made in extra strong and closely woven cotton, resists dirt, grease, and oil. *Spring & Summer 1935*

White back indigo blue denim work pants are Sanforized and have strong triple stitched rip-proof seams. *Spring & Summer 1935*

Nation-Alls in medium and heavy weight fabrics. *Spring & Summer 1935*

"Chieftain" and "Sturdy Oak" work garments are superior in quality. *Spring & Summer 1935*

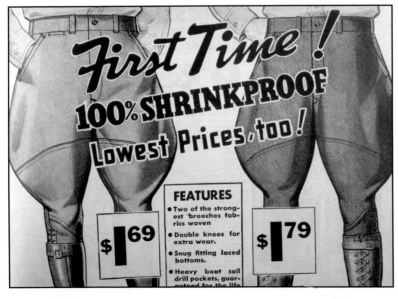

Shrinkproof breeches have double knees, laced bottoms, and generous dimensions. *Spring & Summer 1935*

Coats

"Indestructo" cotton suede cloth jacket is windproof, rainproof, weatherproof. *Spring & Summer 1935*

Officer's style raincoat in waterproof twill has a cotton plaid lining. Buckskein suede cloth coat with check cotton lining. *Fall & Winter 1935-1936*

Heavy weight cotton suede cloth jacket and has a leopard skin pattern cotton fleece lining. *Fall & Winter 1935-1936*

Outerwear

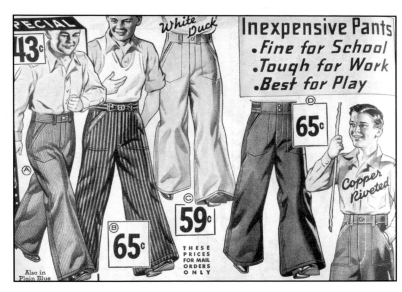

Hercules Jr. heavy duty work suits in white back blue denim. Double Duty Allover suit is big and roomy enough for clothes underneath. *Spring & Summer 1935*

Denim, white duck, and cotton twill pants are fine for school, work, or play. *Spring & Summer 1935*

An assortment of work suits, bibs, and pants for boys. *Spring & Summer 1935*

Shirts

Chieftain Jr., Sturdy Oak Jr., and Hercules work shirts for young men. *Fall & Winter 1935-1936*

Shoes

A variety of canvas sports shoes. *Spring & Summer 1936*

Sports shoes in a variety of styles. *Spring & Summer 1935*

Ventilated white leather uppers with oak-tanned leather sole. Swagger black and white Bal leather upper with oak-tanned leather sole. Wing-Tip white side leather upper with oak-tanned leather sole. *Spring & Summer 1935*

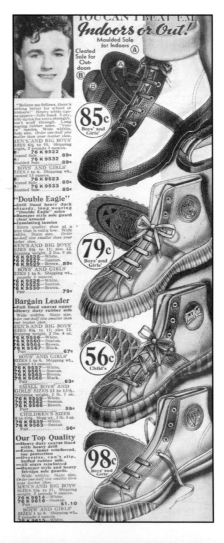

Heavy white canvas uppers with 5-ply built up toe. "Double Eagle" drill lined heavy duck shoes are long wearing. Full lined canvas upper with heavy duty sole. Heavy duty canvas lined shoes with reinforced toe protection. *Fall & Winter 1935-1936*

Slacks

1^{29}

NEW Sanforized Checks

New Shades in Cotton Worsted SLACKS!

Maroon or Royal Blue 1^{35}

Handsome Dark Brown 1^{09}

—PEPPERELL, hard faced, Cotton suiting with fleece back—maroon or royal blue.
—Separate waistband with 1-button extension.
—Pleats in front.. cuff bottoms.
—Two hip pockets.
ALL SIZES: 9 to 18 years. State age-size. Shpg. wt., 1 lb. 1 oz.
40 H 4433 Maroon..... $1.35
40 H 4438 Royal Blue... 1.35

—Strong cotton suiting; broken herringbone weave.
—2-button front with separate waistband.
—Wide cuff bottoms.
—Side buckle straps.
Cool .. because it's cotton! Dark brown; doesn't show the dirt quickly.
ALL SIZES: 9 to 18 years. State age-size. See size scale at right. Shipping wt., 14 oz.
40 H 4455 Dark Brown.. $1.09

Cotton worsted slacks in maroon, royal blue, and dark brown colors. *Spring & Summer 1935*

Boys slacks in gray or brown tweed, navy blue cheviot, and "Window-pane check" cassimere. *Spring & Summer 1935*

Small check black and white heavyweight cotton twill slacks. *Spring & Summer 1935*

1^{89} ← Tweeds

1^{69} 2^{19}

Tweed Cassimere or Cheviot Slacks

$2⁴⁹ $1⁹⁸ $1⁴⁹

Tweed Cassimere or Cheviot slacks
in browns, grays, and navy colors.
Spring & Summer 1935

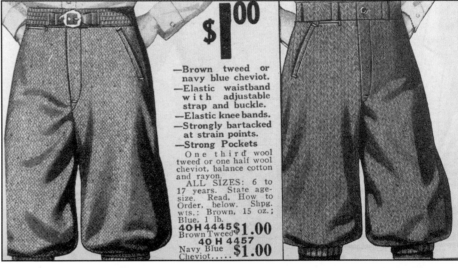

$1⁰⁰

—Brown tweed or
navy blue cheviot.
—Elastic waistband
with adjustable
strap and buckle.
—Elastic knee bands.
—Strongly bartacked
at strain points.
—Strong Pockets
One third wool
tweed or one half wool
cheviot, balance cotton
and rayon.
ALL SIZES: 6 to
17 years. State age-
size. Read, How to
Order, below. Shpg.
wts.: Brown, 15 oz.;
Blue, 1 lb.
40 H 4445 $1.00
Brown Tweed
40 H 4457
Navy Blue
Cheviot..... $1.00

BARGAIN SPECIAL!

94c

—Novelty
weave brown
cotton wor-
sted knickers.
—Extra strong,
full lining.
—Live elastic
bottoms.
—BAR-
TACKED at
all strain
points.
Sears big Spe-
cial! Doesn't
show the dirt.
ALL SIZES: 6
to 14 years.
State age-size.
Read How to
Order, below
Shpg. wt., 1 lb. 1 oz.
40 H 4402
Medium Brown
Lined Knickers
94c

All Wool CASSIMERE

$1⁹⁸

—All wool brown
check CASSI-
MERE or
brown tweed.
—Separate waist-
band with two
buttons.
—Worsted knit
bottoms.
—Full lined.
Our best knickers!
ALL SIZES, 6
to 17 years. State
age-size. Read
How to Order, be-
low.
40 H 4458
Brown all wool
Cassimere. Shpg.
weight,
1 lb. 5 oz. $1.98
40 H 4459
Brown all wool
Tweed. Shipping
weight,
1 lb. 9 oz. $1.98

Knickers in assorted fabrics and styles. *Spring & Summer 1935*

Nub Crash   *Linen*   *Sanforized*

128

Trousers for college youths in tweed, cheviot, or cassimere fabrics. *Spring & Summer 1935*

Topline quality trousers have high waistbands and wide bottoms. *Spring & Summer 1935*

New "ZIP" Slide Fastener Fly

Opens Easily . . .
Always Works . . .
Guaranteed for
Life of Garment

No Bulkiness
. . . Always
Neat Looking
. . . Very Dressy!

Read
"How to
Order" at
Right

Thick corduroy or medium brown window pane check cassimere slacks. *Fall & Winter 1935-1936*

All wool cassimere slacks in a neat check pattern. Handsome cheviot slacks in herringbone weave. *Fall & Winter 1935-1936*

VARSITY
LEADERS for YOUTHS
SIZES 26 to 32-Inch Waist
and 26 to 33-Inch Inseam

Suits

Medium gray all wool Cassimere suit in a neat check pattern. Gray worsted or blue serge all wool double breasted suit. Stylish Cheviot suit in all wool fabric. *Fall & Winter 1934*

Handsome all wool cassimere siut has the latest window pane effect pattern, new fancy checked all wool cassimere suit, all wool cassimere with reversible double breasted vest suit, blue Cheviot suit in subdued Herringbone weave, and the newest style sensation in all virgin wool worsted sport suit. *Spring & Summer 1936*

$7⁹⁵

It Clicked!

That's Why its *Sears*

BEST SELLER!

- **ALL WOOL—** Navy Blue
- **Buttons Sewed With Real Linen Thread**
- **Strong Boat Sail Drill Pockets**

Today's Value **$9⁹⁵**

- Neat Two-Tone Vest
- Pleated Trousers

B **$7⁹⁵**

C 2-Pc. Suit **$4⁹⁸** 3-Pc. Suit **$5⁹⁸**

D 2-Pc. Suit **$4³⁹** 3-Pc. Suit **$5⁴⁹**

Swanky suit with two-tone vest, Navy blue twill weave cheviot, and Brown small check cassimere suits. *Spring & Summer 1935*

All wool navy blue suit with buttons sewed in linen thread. *Spring & Summer 1935*

ALL WOOL and Silk

E
$6 95

F
$7 95

340

see opposite page for des[

All wool and silk cassimere, and navy blue cheviot suits. *Spring & Summer 1935*

ALL WOOL

NEW! *The Free-Swing*
Pleated Patch Pockets – Tattersall Vest

G
One-Pants Suit
$8 45
2-Pants Suit
$10 95

H
$7 98

Free-Swing suits have pleated patch pockets and Tattersall vests.
Spring & Summer 1935

All wool sports back suit in medium brown cassimere. Navy blue or oxford gray cheviot twill weave suit. Both are very stylish. *Spring & Summer 1935*

$9⁹⁵

Here's the NEWEST!

- It's DIFFERENT
- It's STYLISH..
- It's DRESSY...
- And It's *All Wool*

New!
Swagger Vest
Striking new style with snappy welt pockets and fancy pleats. Very latest style.

New!
Sport Back Coat
Very latest model with snappy belted pinch back yoke. Collegiate Style!

New!
Slide Fastener
Modern, handy slide fastener fly! No buttons to bother with! No metal exposed, outside or inside. It's the latest.

The Year's Style Hit!

- All wool. Smooth-finish, Medium Brown Cassimere.
- Two-button, Notch Lapel Model with Shirred Yoke. Full Lined with Lustrous Rayon.
- Wide Bottom Longies with Very Stylish Double Pleats.
- Slide Fastener fly front.
- Overlapping Waistband. Side Buckle Straps.

The very latest campus style. The material drapes handsomely and this sprightly plaid check is a brand new Spring pattern. Wear this suit and lead the style parade.

ALL SIZES: 9 to 18 years. State age-size. See "How to Order" below at left. Shpg. wt., 4 lbs. 3 oz.

40 H 2981—Plaid Check Brown Cassimere ..$9.95

You Are Always WELL DRESSED In a DOUBLE BREASTED

A Proven Value Leader!

- Durable navy blue or oxford gray cheviot twill weave about ⅞ wool.
- Three-button style—peak lapels.
- Full-lined with Rayon.
- Strong twill pocketing.
- Wide cuff bottom longies. Serged seams.

Carefully tailored. No vest. Excellent quality, Sears priced to save you money.

ALL SIZES: 8 to 17 years. State age-size. Shipping

$5⁴⁵

$5.45

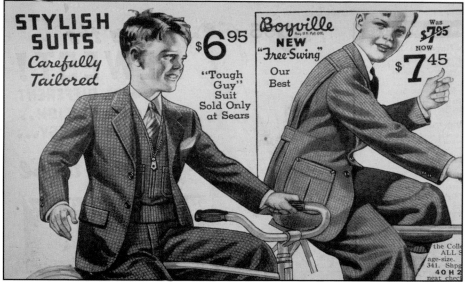

STYLISH SUITS
Carefully Tailored

$6⁹⁵
"Tough Guy" Suit Sold Only at Sears

Boyville
NEW "Free-Swing"
Our Best

Was $7⁹⁵
NOW $7⁴⁵

"Tough Guy" and "Free-Swing" suits are carefully tailored for boys. *Spring & Summer 1935*

Navy Blue or Brown
$4.95

—Sturdy cassimere about ⅞ wool. Reinforced throughout. Bootsail drill pocketing.
—Two-button single breasted, notch lapel coat; full lined with strong Gibraltar lining.
—Slip-over self vest (back same material) slide fastener front, worsted knit bottom.
—Full cut, full lined knickers have worsted knit bottoms. Taped and serged seams.

It's quality all mothers will appreciate. Buttons sewed on with linen thread.

ALL SIZES: 6 to 17 years. State age-size. Read How to Order, Page 341. Shpg. wt., 4 lbs. 1 oz.
40 H 2960—Navy blue check effect
40 H 2961—Medium brown, check effect..$6.95

Read How to Order— on Page 341

SEARS BARGAIN SPECIAL

$3⁷⁹

Smart and stylish suits for boys. *Spring & Summer 1935*

Popular style suits for young collegians. *Spring & Summer 1935*

All wool dark brown cassimere suit has pinch back coat. 2-piece corduroy suit in dark brown or gray. Navy blue cheviot twill weave suit. *Fall & Winter 1935-1936*

Medium brown club check pattern suit. Medium brown check pattern cassimere suit. All wool cassimere suit in new club check pattern. Wool and silk navy blue cheviot suit. *Fall & Winter 1935-1936*

- Center Bellows Pleat; Yoke and Half Belt With Tuck Pleats
- Fine ALL WOOL Suiting in Popular Check Pattern
- Pleated, Cuff-Bottom Trousers

"Free Swing" Action Back (H) **$7⁹⁸**

SEE OPPOSITE PAGE FOR DESCRIPTIONS

IT'S NEW!
Hollywood's Own Style!
- Pleated, Sport Back Hollywood Jacket With Yoke and Half Belt
- Pleated Slacks, Slide Fastener Fly, Wide Cuff Bottoms

2-Piece Outfit **$5⁴⁵** (G)

Last Fall **$8⁴⁵**

Wool and Silk

Pleated Slacks Slide Fastener Front

263

New Hollywood style comes in this smooth finish cassimere suit. Window pane check pattern on a medium brown wool and silk cassimere suit. *Fall & Winter 1935-1936*

REVERSIBLE VEST SUIT **$8⁹⁵**

Full o' Pep!
and Bargain Priced

EASY PAYMENTS now offered on Men's Suits and Overcoats. See Easy Payment Page in back of catalog for Terms.

(C) **$11⁵⁰** Blue Serge

(D) **$9⁹⁵** All Wool

Dark blue all wool cheviot, all wool cassimere in window pane checked pattern, all wool blue serge, all wool blue cheviot, dark brown cassimere, and all wool cassimere suits for young men. *Fall & Winter 1935-1936*

Collegiate fashion in dark blue check wool and silk, one-button single breasted peak lapel, form fitting coat, and wide cuff bottoms. *Fall & Winter 1935-1936*

Sweaters

All Wool Heavy Shaker
$1⁸⁹

—Heavyweight yarns.
—Sturdy Shaker Stitch.
—Popular V neck style.

There's warmth in every inch and wear in every stitch. You can't match this quality at anywhere near the price. Snug fitting cuffs and bottom. Heavyweight shaker stitch assures lasting wear and comfortable fit.

83 K 1740—Navy Blue
83 K 1742—Black $1.89

Even sizes 26 to 36 inches chest. State size. Shipping weight, 1 lb. 10 oz.

Warm and Stylish
95c

—Narrow gauge shaker stitch.
—Strong, about 50% wool yarns.
—Military collar. Talon opening.

Compare features—then compare price. Here's a big value. A medium heavy weight that's built for warmth, wear and comfortable fit.

83 K 1883—Navy Blue
83 K 1884—Maroon
83 K 1885—Tan   95c

Even sizes 28 to 36 inches chest. State size. Shipping weight, 12 oz.

Former Price $~~2³⁵~~ $1⁹⁸

All wool heavy Shaker sweater. Half wool Shaker sweater with Talon opening. Indestructo fleeced cotton back suede cloth Cossack jacket. *Fall & Winter 1935-1936*

IT'S ALL WOOL

Popular Style and Price
95c

—Sturdy All Wool Yarns.
—Heavy Cardigan Stitch.
—Excellent workmanship.

Styled for looks and built for wear. You'll look smart with the snappy contrasting trim at neck, cuffs and bottom. Made exceptionally strong . . priced exceptionally low. A real Sears bargain! Shipping weight, 11 ounces.

83 K 1748—Navy, with contrasting trim.
83 K 1749—Maroon with contrasting trim.

Even sizes 26 to 36 inches chest. State size.

Refer to page 345 for Measuring Instructions.

All wool sweaters in popular styles. *Fall & Winter 1935-1936*

Undergarments

Suits for boys with button up fronts or shoulder button styles.
Spring & Summer 1935

Pilgrim and Boyville part wool union suits. *Fall & Winter 1935-1936*

Boys Fashions

Coats

All wool Melton cloth windbreaker in the new Cossack style. Cotton suede jacket in new Cossack style. Medium-weight Navy Blue Melton cloth in Cossack style. *Spring & Summer 1935*

All Wool Windbreaker

- ALL WOOL melton cloth.
- Double stitched, strong seams.
- New Cossack style. Slide fastener front. Button tab on collar.
- Big, deep muff style pockets.
- Side buckle straps. Button cuffs.

A boy needs a warm jacket nearly all year 'round! Girls wear this style, too! Warm medium weight. No buttons to button . . . closes with a zip! He can turn the collar up to keep his neck warm. It's full cut for growing boys. Our price is certainly exceptional for this most excellent quality. Compare this jacket with the higher priced ones offered elsewhere.

EVEN SIZES: 6 to 16 yrs. State age-size.

Shipping weight, 1 lb. 12 oz.

40 H 3592
Navy Blue....................$2.19

40 H 3593
Maroon $2.19

WINDPROOF WATERPROOF

$2.19

$2.35

$1.79

From suits to coats, these styles for young boys will keep in fashion. *Fall & Winter 1934*

Hats

Hats for boys of all ages.
Spring & Summer 1935

Sheepskin leather hat with cotton flannel lining. Genuine DuPont fabrikoid racing hat with warm cotton lining. Horsehide hat with cotton lining. *Fall & Winter 1935-1936*

Pajamas

One- and two-piece pajamas for boys in short and long styles. *Spring & Summer 1935*

Cotton flannel pajamas in assorted styles. *Fall & Winter 1935-1936*

Dr. Denton's nationally known sleeping garments. *Fall & Winter 1935-1936*

Big and roomy pajamas and robe for boys. *Fall & Winter 1935-1936*

Play Clothes

"Heap Big Chief", 4-piece baseball set, "Wild Westerner", and "Texas Ranger" play outfits for young boys. *Spring & Summer 1936*

Sturdy Oak, Jr. and Hercules Jr. are two fine choices in overalls for the younger man. *Spring & Summer 1936*

"Sky Rider", "Big Leaguer", leather chaps, corduroy cotton khaki twill pants, "Heap Big Injun", white cotton jeans and sweat shirt, "Rodeo Rider", blue cotton covert or khaki cotton jean, and a cowboy outfit are all fine choices for play clothes for a boy. *Spring & Summer 1934*

Cut over full, roomy patterns. All seams are reinforced and covered where the wear comes. No raw edges.

Boy's playsuits in hickory stripe or plain blue colors. *Fall & Winter 1934*

Be Modern! Let your Kiddies dress themselves in **Self-Help** CLOTHES
Make them self-reliant — save you time! Approved by doctors and child specialists

B It pays to buy good Cotton Broadcloth like this!

No Button Drop Seat

C

$1.00

Made Easy!

s! No Buttons little fingers!

of mothers who have bought ...es for their children! Up-to-...raise their convenience, their ...s. Easy drop seats and front ...ke children independent and ...or night!

...ELP PANTY DRESS
...washfast cotton print, with easy ...-fastener down front. Well cut ...nt. Ages, 2, 3, 4, 5, 6 yrs. State ...plaids.............. **$1.29**

...IECE SUIT
...ton Broadcloth. No button Drop ...belt. Talon hookless fastener ...broidery trim on collar. Ages, 1, ...age. Shpg. wt., 5 oz. **$1.00**
38 H 5459—Green..

...ON COVERT PLAY SUIT
...Drop seat. Talon slide front. ...pockets. Cuff bottoms. Ages, 2, ...e age. Shpg. wt., 8 oz. **$1.00**
38 H 6127—Tan ..

TALON FEATHERWEIGHT SLIDE FASTENERS
ELIMINATE BUTTON TROUBLE
CANNOT RUST
ALWAYS WORK
LAUNDER PERFECTLY

$1.00 SUIT

Hard to Wear Out

Boys' "Self-Help" one-piece suit in cotton broadcloth. Boys' sturdy cotton playsuit. *Spring & Summer 1935*

Husky Well Made PLAY SUITS
39c

(A) Dirt and rough-and-tumble play won't hurt this suit! Made of a good quality washable Chambray. Long legs; drop seat. Buttons down front. Red piping.
Ages: 1, 2, 3, 4, 5, 6 yrs. State age-size. Shipping weight, 6 ounces.
38 H 6115—Blue

Chambray

(B) (C) **45c EACH**

Husky Chambray play suits. *Spring & Summer 1935*

(B) **Choice of Two Serviceable Materials.** Stoutly made, well-sewed, playsuits. Double needle seams throughout. Drop seat. Open down front. Ages: 2, 3, 4, 5, 6, 7 yrs. State age. Shpg. wt. 8 oz.
38 H 6154—Blue Pinstripe
38 H 6155 Hickory Stripe **45c**

(C) **Chambray—Serviceable**
Strong Peg Top play suit. Good quality chambray that will stand soap and water and come out looking fresh and new! Opens down back. Five-button drop seat.
Ages: 2, 3, 4, 5, 6, 7 yrs. State age. Shpg. wt., 7 oz.
38 H 6152—Blue
38 H 6153—Green **45c**

Self Help Drop Seat

Well M
Two-Pie
Dapper we
suit with co
pants, novelt
cotton broadc
Ages: 1, 2
State age-s
wt., 6 oz.
38 H 545
with yellow
38 H 545
Blue with whit

(D) **CHAMBRAY OR COVERT**

↑ **59c**

(D) **A New Play Suit**
Choice of two serviceable, better quality, heavyweight cotton fabrics. Gay Turkey Red piping on collar and cuffs and fancy pockets. Buttons down front. "Self-Help" drop seat. Suits will wear and wear. Ages: 1, 2, 3, 4, 5, 6 years. State age. Shpg. wt., 7 oz.
38 H 6120—Blue Chambray
38 H 6121 Blue Covert **59c**

(E) **2-Piece Overall Style Play Suit.** Good quality cotton covert cloth. Tailored overalls with blouse that can be worn inside or out, with Talon hookless fastener and wide elastic at waist to prevent riding up. Adjustable straps on overall.
Ages: 2, 3, 4, 5, 6 yrs. State age. Shpg. wt., 9 oz.
38 H 6104—Tan
38 H 6105—Blue
38 H 6106—Green **98c**

(E) **98c**

Covert

Sears NEW Play-Costume Outfits

(A) **8-Piece Outfit $1.98**

(B) **Outfit With Vest $1.00**

(C) **Bargain Special $1.35 8 Pieces**

(D) **8-Piece Outfit $2.59**

"Rodeo Rider," "Dude Rancher," "Broncho Buster," and "Stage Coach Dan" play-costume outfits. *Spring & Summer 1935*

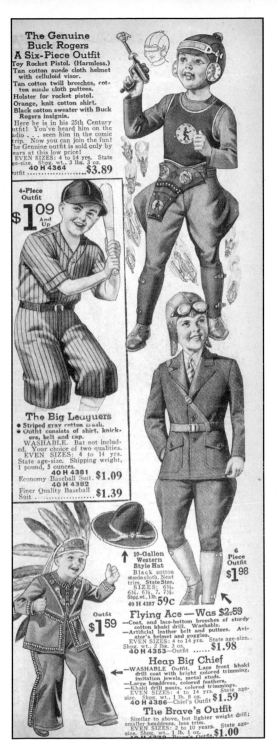

Far left:
"Buck Rogers" six-piece outfit, "The Big Leaguers" four-piece, "Flying Ace," and "Heap Big Chief" play outfits for boys. *Spring & Summer 1935*

Top right:
Play suits are blue denim in solids or stripes. *Spring & Summer 1935*

Bottom right:
Blazer longie suit in blue twill weave cheviot. Navy blue corduroy Cossack jacket and pants set. Sailor suit with suspenders includes blue and white striped cotton shirt. *Fall & Winter 1935-1936*

147

Big Pal or Hercules play suits.
Fall & Winter 1935-1936

Cowboy, Texas Ranger, and two Buck
Jones play suits. *Fall & Winter 1935-1936*

Shirts

EACH 21c EACH

Deep Blue Dress Shirts
74c EACH
- Excellent quality cotton broadcloth • Newest spring style • Strongly tailored
Here's the same rich navy blue dress shirt men are wearing at a low cost. Coat style.
33 H 1435—Deep Blue
JUVENILE SIZES: Ages 6, 8, 10, 12 years. State age. Shipping weight, 7 oz.
BOYS' SIZES: 12½ to 14½ in. neck. Half sizes. State size. Shipping weight, 9 ounces.

Smart New Patterns
—Colorful rayon fabrics; lined ends
—Four-in-hand styles
An extra big tie purchase cut price in two. Why not buy four or five when they cost so little? Smart patterns and handsome fabrics the boy is proud to wear.
33 H 8560—Plain Colors
33 H 8561—Fancy Patterns
Both come in Blue, Red, Green, Brown, Purple or Green. State color. Shipping weight, 3 ounces.

EACH 79c Were 89c

Price Reduced Again
- Fine quality lustrous cotton broadcloth
- Plain colors are pre-shrunk
- Collar and cuffs interlined for better fit
- Government standard size specifications
- Vat dyed fadeproof colors
- Fancy patterns not pre-shrunk
- Fine quality buttons
- Beautifully tailored

Priced much higher in many stores. Cut styled and tailored like a man's shirt. They have that "silky" feel and finish men buy. Better yarns spun into a finer weave. Coat style. Ties not included.
33 H 1450—Plain White   33 H 1452—Plain Blue
33 H 1451—Plain Tan   33 H 1453—Plain Green
33 H 1455—Fancy patterns (not pre-shrunk)
JUVENILE SIZES: Ages, 6, 8, 10, 12 years. State age. Shpg. wt., 7 oz.
BOYS' SIZES: 12½ to 14½ in. neck. Half sizes. State size. Shpg. wt., 9 oz.

SEARS BARGAIN SPECIALS...

Police Style Suspender 25c
—Live strong elastic webbing.
—Leather ends.
—Nickel plated steel fittings.
—32 in. long.
Styled like Dad's for hard wear.
Price Cut!
33 H 8762
Shpg. wt., 4 ounces.

Plain or Fancy Shirts
59c EACH Were 65c
- Plain colors in genuine cotton broadcloth
- Fancy Patterns in cotton shirtings.
- Fast Colors.
- Laundered Beautifully.
A wide selection of bright colors and fancy patterns in excellent quality cotton shirtings. Roomy sizes. Coat style. Tie not included.
33 H 5020—Plain White
33 H 5021—Plain Tan
33 H 5023—Plain Blue
33 H 5022—Plain Green
33 H 5024—Fancy Patterns
JUVENILE SIZES: Ages, 6, 8, 10, 12 years. State age. Shipping weight, 7 ounces.
BOYS' SIZES: 12½ to 14½ inches neck. Half sizes. State size. Shipping weight, 9 ounces.

25c Boys' Dress Suspender
—Rayon Elastic Webbing.
—Pearl gray leather ends.
—Colored designs.
—Standard 32-inch length.
One of the smartest models ever designed for a boy.
33 H 8766
Shipping weight, 3 ounces

Plain or Fancy 43c EACH
—Sturdy, firmly woven cotton shirtings
—Government standard size dimensions
—Large assortment of new fancy patterns and plain colors.
You'd find it hard to pass up this price if you could see what thoroughly good shirtings these are. Not skimped in a single detail. Sears standard quality dress shirts, carefully tailored. Regular collar attached coat style. Strong buttons. Tie not included.
33 H 1436—Plain White
33 H 1437—Plain Tan
33 H 1438—Plain Blue
33 H 1438—Fancy Patterns
JUVENILE SIZES: 6, 8, 10, 12 years. State age. Shipping weight, 7 ounces.
BOYS' SIZES: 12½ to 14½ inches neck measure. Half sizes. State size. Shipping weight, 9 ounces.

Boys' Sport Shirt 43c EACH
—Sport collar
—Short sleeves
—Excellent quality cotton shirtings
—Cut over Government standard specifications
—Coat style
—Newest plain colors and fancy patterns
Show us the boy who doesn't look smarter, cooler, happier in a fresh sportster like this. Show us a price low for such satisfactory quality. Roomy sizes. Strongly tailored throughout.
33 H 1440—Plain White
33 H 1441—Plain Tan
33 H 1442—Plain Blue
33 H 1443—Fancy Patterns
JUVENILE SIZES: 6, 8, 10 and 12 years. State age-size. Shipping weight, 6 oz.
BOYS' SIZES: 12½ to 14½ inches neck measure. Half sizes. State size. Shipping weight, 8 ounces.

Genuine Cowhide Leather 21c
—Fancy grain genuine cowhide leather
—Smart nickel plated tongue buckle
—Practical 1¼-inch width
Attractive, durable belt. Will give your boy a lot of good dependable service.
33 H 8881—Black
33 H 8884—Grey
Even sizes, 24 to 36 inches waist measure. State size wanted. Shipping weight, 4 ounces.

Low Priced White Sport Belt 35c
—Full grain cowhide bridle leather
—Attractive striped patterns.
—Nickel plated buckle.
Matches any 50c boys' belt we ever saw! We can't buy belts we ever price. Ideal for new! stylish summer outfits
33 H 8895—White with Black Stripes.
33 H 8896—White with Brown Stripes.
Even sizes, 24 to 30 inches. State size. Shpg. wt., 4 oz.

Silver Plated Buckle ... Was 49c 39c
—Full grain cowhide bridle leather
—Beautifully embossed slide buckle
—Width, about 1¼ inches
A splendid boys' belt made like the more expensive young men's model. Any boy would be proud to own it. Extra strong and durable.
33 H 8890—Black
33 H 8892—Light   33 H 8891—Grey

328   prices in this Sears catalog are

Shirts in plain or fancy styles, ties, belts, and suspenders for boys.
Spring & Summer 1935

Hercules work shirts for boys in pre-shrunk medium-weight chambray or khaki cotton.
Spring & Summer 1935

Medium-weight pullover with genuine Talon-slide fastener. Sporty medium-weight sweater has sporty trim at neck, cuffs, and bottom. All wool worsted vest has fancy stitch with snug fitting bottom. *Spring & Summer 1935*

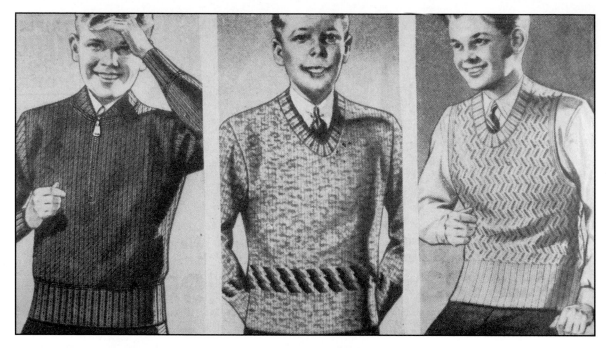

All wool napped sweater with Talon slide fastener and military collar. All wool medium-weight sweater with contrasting Jacquard trim. Cotton sweater has an attractive pineapple stitch and talon slide fastener. *Spring & Summer 1935*

Shoes

Brown chrome tanned leather hi-cut boots has a pocket on right shoe for coins or keys. Shoes of durable leather uppers are long wearing. *Fall & Winter 1935-1936*

Boys chocolate color boots have rawhide laces, and genuine Goodyear welt. *Fall & Winter 1935-1936*

Moccasin style oxfords with genuine Goodyear welts in brown or black.
Fall & Winter 1935-1936

Suits & Dressy Outfits

Knicker suits for boys in nubbed cassimere, Herringbone weave cassimere, Herringbone weave Cheviot, and Herringbone weave cassimere. *Spring & Summer 1934*

Two tone corduroy outfit in navy or burgundy brown, all wool pure worsted knit bottoms in brown or gray, and stylish tweed in gray or brown. *Spring & Summer 1934*

Very, very 1936 styles for young men tailored in all wool and silk.
Spring & Summer 1936

Sports suits in the season's most popular styles. *Spring & Summer 1936*

Five-piece outfit includes longies, cotton broadcloth blouse, rayon necktie, wool jersey jacket, and self belt. Brown or Navy Blue suit in half wool Cheviot fabric. *Spring & Summer 1935*

Five-piece Cheviot suits in navy blue twill weave.
Spring & Summer 1935

Shorts or longie outfits in button on style tan cotton broadcloth.
Spring & Summer 1935

Easy to wash and iron camp suits.
Spring & Summer 1935

Big Savings on
Juvenile Suits
for Boys from
2 to 10 Years

Half Belt
Pinch Back
Coat

$2³⁹

Juvenile suits for boys 2-10 years old
in assorted styles and fabrics. *Spring
& Summer 1935*

French spun all wool worsted jersey brother and sister suits. *Fall & Winter 1935-1936*

4-piece rugby suit in navy blue half wool cheviot. 5-piece blue twill weave cheviot suit. *Fall & Winter 1935-1936*

A selection of suits and snow suits for young boys. *Fall & Winter 1935-1936*

Ties

Comic character silk crepe ties for boys. *Fall & Winter 1935-1936*

Catalog Pages Used

Spring & Summer 1934
Pages18, 20, 35, 45, 63, 73, 86, 234, 237, 264, 283, 327, 344, 348, 353, 359.

Fall & Winter 1934
Pages 8, 10, 16, 17, 39, 41, 42, 49, 50, 55, 61, 63, 80, 84, 102, 134, 135, 137, 273, 276, 299, 308, 333, 379, 386, 422, 425, 435, 447, 454, 457.

Spring & Summer 1935
Pages 6, 8, 12, 13, 15, 17, 19, 21, 22, 23, 27, 31, 38, 39, 40, 41, 43, 44, 47, 48, 51, 52, 53, 55, 57, 59, 60, 61, 62, 63, 64, 65, 67, 69, 70, 72, 73, 74, 75, 77, 78, 81, 84, 85, 91, 92, 93, 95, 99, 103, 109, 116, 117, 121, 122, 123, 124, 125, 242, 246, 247, 248, 251, 254, 255, 256, 258, 259, 262, 265, 266, 268, 272, 274, 275, 280, 282, 288, 289, 290, 292, 293, 295, 296, 299, 303, 305, 307, 308, 311, 313, 315, 316, 326, 327, 328, 329, 330, 332, 333, 334, 335, 336, 337, 338, 339, 340, 341, 342, 343, 344, 345, 346, 347, 348, 349, 350, 353, 354, 356, 358, 359, 360, 361, 364, 365, 366, 367, 368, 369, 372, 373, back cover.

Fall & Winter 1935-1936
Pages 6, 8, 10, 11, 12, 13, 15, 17, 18, 22, 23, 24, 25, 27, 29, 31, 33, 35, 36, 38, 39, 40, 41, 42, 43, 44, 45, 46, 49, 50, 51, 53, 54, 55, 57, 62, 63, 65, 66, 67, 70, 71, 72, 73, 75, 77, 80, 83, 86, 87, 90, 97, 98, 122, 123, 125, 126, 129, 130, 132, 137, 138, 141, 142, 143, 145, 147, 150, 159, 163, 164, 167, 171, 178, 181, 183, 185, 187, 189, 192, 195, 203, 206, 211, 227, 246, 251, 256, 258, 262, 263, 264, 269, 270, 272, 273, 275, 280, 295, 297, 298, 303, 307, 308, 309, 316, 317, 319, 321, 322, 331, 333, 334, 335, 336, 337, 339, 341, 343, 344, 347, 348, 349, 359, 363, 365, 372.

Spring & Summer 1936
Pages 6, 12, 18, 23, 24, 25, 26, 27, 33, 35, 36, 37, 41, 44, 47, 49, 57, 71, 75, 96, 113, 142, 144, 161, 175, 188, 221, 230, 236, 243, 253, 254, 256.